THE BORDER COLLIE

Tracy Libby

Project Team
Editor: Cynthia P. Gallagher
Copy Editor: Ann Fusz
Design: Angela Stanford
Series Design: Mada Design and Stephanie Krautheim
Series Originator: Dominique De Vito

T.F.H. Publications
President/CEO: Glen S. Axelrod
Executive Vice President: Mark E. Johnson
Publisher: Christopher T. Reggio
Production Manager: Kathy Bontz

T.F.H. Publications, Inc.
One TFH Plaza
Third and Union Avenues
Neptune City, NJ 07753

06 07 08 09 10 1 3 5 7 9 8 6 4 2
Printed and bound in China
Library of Congress Cataloging-in-Publication Data
   Libby, Tracy, 1958-
    The Border collie / Tracy Libby.
      p. cm.
    Includes index.
    ISBN 0-7938-3676-X (alk. paper)
    1. Border collie. I. Title.
    SF429.B64L53 2006
    636.737'4--dc22
   2006017805

This book has been published with the intent to provide accurate and authoritative information in regard to the subject matter within. While every precaution has been taken in preparation of this book, the author and publisher expressly disclaim responsibility for any errors, omissions, or adverse effects arising from the use or application of the information contained herein. The techniques and suggestions are used at the reader's discretion and are not to be considered a substitute for veterinary care. If you suspect a medical problem consult your veterinarian.

The Leader In Responsible Animal Care For Over 50 Years.™
www.tfh.com

TABLE OF CONTENTS

HISTORY

of the Border Collie

Border Collies have been declared the most intelligent dogs on the planet. In fact, it's been said that they are so smart, they can pick your pockets clean and leave you smiling about it. Picking pockets may be a good side gig, but their day job is premier sheepdog. They are the working stiffs of the herding world, and they live it morning 'til night.

Border Collies have been bred for hundreds of years with one goal in mind: supreme herding ability. Unmatched in their brains, instinct, and endurance, they can do just about anything—and do it first rate. The Border Collie's intelligence, trainability, agility, and relentless energy have made him a favorite in all areas of canine ownership because experienced handlers make training and showing them look like a stroll in the park. The breed's bread and butter, however, is also its curse because the very qualities that make them top notch sheepdogs frequently make them unsuitable as pets. Border Collies differ from other dogs, and owning one is not like owning any other breed of dog. They are highly complex animals, and to understand and truly appreciate this remarkable breed, you must first understand its early history, origin, and the function for which they were originally bred.

BORDER COLLIES IN HISTORY

Herding dogs have been around for thousands of years, perhaps as many as 14,000 years according to some accounts, but no one knows for certain when they were first trained to earn their keep herding sheep or working for man. Biblical references, such as Job 30:1 refer to dogs with flocks.

Roman scholars such as Marcus Terentius Varro (116 BCE–27 BCE) wrote about the care and training of shepherd dogs, as well as a sheepdog he procured as a watchdog. He noted the dog should be "large, with a deep bark, and white in color so as to be more easily recognized in the dark." Others, including Xenophon, an early pupil of Socrates (430-355 BCE), Greek philosopher Aristotle (384-322 BCE), and

Dogs have served humankind as sheepherders for millennia; there are literary references dating back to over 400 years BCE.

Greek historian Flavius Arrianus (CE 85-150), were a few of the many early writers who also wrote about dogs.

The earliest herding dogs, in all probability, descended from guard dogs similar to those that accompanied the Romans when they invaded Britain in CE 43. Back then, no means of refrigeration existed, so meat for the soldiers traveled on the hoof. These large, courageous, and intelligent drover-type dogs transported or "drove" livestock to market. They were a collection of canines of every size, shape, and color and were utilized for their proficiency at herding livestock, as well as protecting the camp from marauders. These dogs would undoubtedly have been crossed—intentionally or unintentionally— with other dogs, perhaps including the herding spitz- type dogs belonging to the Vikings, invaders of Britain between the eighth and ninth centuries. The theory being that these breedings most likely produced smaller, more active and agile, working dogs. The wool industry was essential to the British economy, and it's highly likely the hill shepherds would have valued these active, agile dogs for herding. Over time, shepherds, ranchers, and farmers would have selectively bred these dogs to suit their particular needs.

Many historians assume this to be true; although much of it is based on speculation and still open to dispute. People like to have their histories neat and tidy, but truth be told, there is much we do not know about the early history and origin of collies, sheepdogs, and Border Collies. Just as we may never know for certain whether George Washington really cut down the infamous cherry tree or threw a dollar over the Delaware River, we may, unfortunately, never know for certain the earliest and true origin of the modern-day dog we know and love as the Border Collie.

BORDER COLLIES IN THE BORDER COUNTRY

What historians know for certain is that the Border Collie we know today developed in the border land between England, Scotland, and Wales. Of course, 150 years ago most breeds of dogs were not clearly defined, and the Border Collie was simply known as a collie, sheepdog, or shepherd's dog.

One of the earliest writings of working sheepdogs in Britain was Dr. John Caisus' 1570 book, *Treatise on Englishe Dogges*. Caisus, the physician-in-chief to Queen Elizabeth I, described the working style of sheepdogs of his day. Interestingly, his description written more than 400 years ago bears an uncanny resemblance to the working style of today's Border Collies. With apologies to historians and traditionalists, the old passage and its quaint spelling has been modernized for today's reader, as quoted from Rawdon Lee's 1890 book *A History and Description of the Collie or Sheep Dog in His British Varieties*. "This dog, either at the hearing of his master's voice or at the wagging of his fist, or at his shrill and hoarse whistling and hissing, bringeth the wandering wethers and straying sheep into the self- same place where his master's will and work is to have them, whereby the shepherd reapeth this benefit, namely, that with little labour and no toil or moving of his feet he may rule and guide his flock according to his own desire, either to have them go forward or stand still, or to draw backward, or to turn this way or to take that way."

In the 1700s and early 1800s, the works of Thomas Bewick and James Hogg appeared. Bewick's 1790 book *A General History of Quadrupeds* includes an engraving of a Shepherd's Dog. Hogg, a shepherd and poet from the Ettrick Valley in the Scottish Borders, wrote "without him [the sheep dog] the mountainous land of England and Scotland would not be worth sixpence. It would require more hands to manage a flock of sheep and drive them to market than the profits of the whole were capable of maintaining." Hogg also wrote about his own two collies, describing their stalking behaviors and the characteristic "eye"—the "intense gaze" that gives a Border Collie the power to hold, control, and move livestock—that closely resemble the behaviors present in today's Border Collies.

Border Collie Names

Traditionalists like to maintain the shepherd's custom of giving their working Border Collies short names, such as Mick, Bess, Nell, Glen, Meg, and Tweed. These short names can easily be shouted on a windy hillside, and as practical folk, shepherds don't have a lot of time for fancy names. As the Border Collie's popularity as a companion dog and agility and obedience competitor has increased, so too has the diversity of names. Upbeat names, such as Flash, Luke, Tex, and Rio, as well as multi-syllable names including Bronco, Twister, and Striker, are not uncommon. While the names may offend the ears and good senses of shepherds and long time sheep dog enthusiasts, the names are not at all out of place on the agility course or in the obedience ring.

During the mid-to-late 1800s and early 1900s, Britain, Scotland, Wales, Ireland, and France had scores of different breeds of pastoral dogs including Scotch Collies, Highland Collies, Dorset Blue Shags, Smithfield Sheepdogs, Cumberland Sheepdogs, Glenwherry Collies, and Welsh Greys. Nearly every county or shire had a separate strain of pastoral dog, and each one was developed and used for a particular purpose and to suit the needs of the situation. Welsh Greys, for instance, were especially good at working large groups of feral goats. Dorset Sheepdogs were used to manage the difficult and aggressive Portland sheep that frequently attacked and butted the dogs. Smithfield dogs were used for driving cattle long distances from the marshes to the Smithfield Meat Markets in London. Shepherds and their strain of collies from the Highlands and Lowlands of Scotland, known as the "Woburn pack", were employed on the estates of the Dukes of Bedford. Another strain from the North country, known as "Lordie's" or "Laudie's pups" were used on the estates of Earls of Lonsdale. Historians believe these dogs were cross-bred, intentionally or unintentionally, to strengthen desired features and produce better working dogs.

Many of the old breeds are now extinct, but they played a significant and important role in contributing to the genetic pool of contemporary pastoral dogs we know today, including Border Collies, Australian Shepherds, Rough and Smooth Collies, and McNabs. These contemporary working dogs, including your Border Collie, came from

Though not distinguished as a true Border Collie long ago, the shepherd dogs that worked the Border Country had the "eye" and stalking behavior characteristic of today's Border Collies.

the general genetic pool of working collies / sheepdogs. It just took a while for today's breed distinctions to be developed.

In England, the Border Collie emerged as the dominant herding dog. Many of these dogs, according to Sheila Grew's book, *Key Dogs From the Border Collie Family*, were hard and powerful, often rough with stock and difficult to control, but their keen instinct, concentration, and great power over sheep made it worth trying to breed a milder-natured type dog.

Border Collies remained strictly working sheepdogs until the 1860s—their working skill and ability superseding all other requirements, such as physical appearance, size, and color. Remember, however, at that time, they were not yet known as Border Collies, but simply collies or sheepdogs. Several events propelled the collie dog's popularity, including the first official dog show that took place at Newcastle-on-Tyne in 1859. Rumor has it that Queen Victoria first saw the rough-coated collies at Balmoral Castle in the highlands of Scotland and took an instant liking to them, which quickly elevated them to royal status. Owning one became fashionable, and they were given a class at the newly formed dog shows. Queen Victoria's own dog was shown in the early 1860s, and breed historians say the dog could easily pass today for a pedigreed Border Collie.

Shepherds in Britain provided most of the collies entered in early dog shows, but they quickly realized they would be toying with disaster if they tried to breed a dual-purpose dog for both show points and working ability. This was a critical juncture for the Border Collie we know and love today.

Dog show enthusiasts, on the other hand, continued showing their dogs, presumably crossing their collie dogs with the Russian Wolfhound, as well as other breeds. The name "shepherd" became associated with the blunt-nosed, heavy-eared working dog and the "collie" name with the narrow-headed, higher-eared kennel-club registered dog.

The advent of sheep dog trials in 1873 and the formation of the International Sheep Dog Society in 1906, perhaps more so than any other events, helped to stimulate interest in the shepherd, improve the skill of handlers, and establish the Border Collie's modern heritage through concentrated and selective breeding programs that favored the quality of "eye" and the overriding importance of working style, ability and durability. Prior to the much-publicized herding trials, dogs

Spot 1

In the early 1920s, Sam Stoddart, a Scottish shepherd who had immigrated to America, returned to his native land and purchased the 1923 Supreme Champion "Spot." Spot, later to be known as Spot 1, sired many great dogs in this country and is considered by many to be the forerunner of the present day Border Collie in America.

tended to be rougher, pushier, and more difficult to control. Breeders quickly recognized that dogs with more finesse tended to win the herding trials, so they began breeding for dogs with a stronger eye and more biddable—trainable or controllable—nature. The first notable dog of that type was Hemp, also known as Old Hemp, born in 1894. His dam was a strong-eyed dog; his, sire a dog more of the original type: powerful, loose-eyed, and pushy. Old Hemp is considered the founder of the modern Border Collie breed. Interestingly, the title "old" refers not to the dog's age, but as a way to help identify a dog who is named after is sire (or dam).

THE BORDER COLLIE IN AMERICA

As immigrants began flooding into North America during the mid-to-late 1800s and early 1900s, so too did their dogs, and many of these fine dogs from the British Isles found their way to America. Old turn-of-the-century photographs show dogs resembling Border Collies posed or working with western homesteaders, ranchers, farmers, and families.

A photo from the 1890s shows the author's great-grandmother with a collie/ shepherd dog.

In 1848 the California Gold Rush caused a mass migration of people moving westward to California's gold country in search of an easy fortune. San Francisco's population exploded from a mere 1,000 in 1848 to 20,000 by 1850. The flood of people created an increased need for mutton and wool for food and clothing. As a result, large flocks of sheep were driven from the Midwest and New Mexico to California. Dogs accompanying the large flocks would have been mostly old-fashioned collie-type

dogs or shepherd dogs who came to America with settlers from the British Isles.

Scotsmen from the border country understood the value of a good herding dog. When they began immigrating to America during the mid-to-late 19th century, they brought with them their working collies. This was no small task, considering it was years before the advent of jet airplanes that today whisk us across the Atlantic in a matter of hours. Their journey by ship would have taken considerably longer and most likely was fraught with hardship and peril.

One such notable immigrant was Andrew Little, a Scotsman who arrived in Caldwell, Idaho in 1894 with his two Scotch Collies, Kate and Jim. In his native Scotland, Little herded the family's band of sheep over the heather-clad hills from Moffat to the trade center of Glasgow. At the age of 24, seeking a better life in America, Little emigrated and became an integral part of the American west by developing the largest sheep operation in Idaho, and perhaps in the entire nation. At the prime of his operation, Little had hundreds of fully trained Border Collies working a 7,000 square mile boundary where more than 300,000 sheep ranged. Little's dogs were versatile: they herded, guarded, protected, and obeyed the herder's commands. Little, who had a reputation with dogs, imported additional dogs from Scotland. These black and white dogs had the familiar Border Collie names: Jim, Kate, and Tweed.

It is worth noting that in the years leading up to the 1900s, specific breeds were not as clearly defined as they are today, and much interbreeding of the various strains of herding dogs would have taken place. Good working dogs were bred to other good working dogs. Pedigrees and physical appearances seldom factored into the equation. In 1894 these dogs were probably not called Border Collies but were simply referred to as Scotch collies, working collies, or sheepdogs. It's possible they were very similar dogs to what we know today as Border Collies, but prior to the 20th century dog breeds were not as clearly separated as they are now.

Basques were among the first Europeans to immigrate to America, coming from their homeland where the western range of the Pyrenees meets the Bay of Biscay and forms part of the border between France and Spain. Unlike the Scotsmen, it was not as common for Basques to immigrate with their dogs because genuine Basque sheepherders did not immigrate. Most Basques immigrating to America sought a better life, but not specifically as sheepherders.

Old Hemp

Old Hemp was bred by Northumbrian farmer Adam Telfer. He was the result of breeding the hard, rough, powerful but difficult-to-control dogs with milder-natured collies. He was the first Border Collie registered in Britain with the International Sheep Dog Society. He is considered by many to be the father of the modern Border Collie breed.

Scotch and Basque immigrants were the first to use Border Collies in America.

Wiston Cap

Wiston Cap, born in 1963, is considered the modern father of the Border Collie breed. He had a significant and permanent influence on the breed in the mid-1900s. He was the most popular stud dog in the breed's history, producing many top-winning offspring and was the 1965 International Champion.

They learned new trades including shepherding, and in true Basque tradition, they became masters at whatever trade they tackled. Most Basque sheepherders would have purchased, traded, or acquired dogs from other shepherds who had earlier immigrated to California, Oregon, Nevada, and Idaho. Some would have acquired dogs from other neighbors, farmers, or ranchers, like Andy Little, who employed their services.

Like the Scotsmen, the Basques were often paid in land and sheep, and they too began to make their mark on America. Dominique Laxalt was one of them, emigrating from France to Nevada in 1906 with little but the shirt on his back. At the height of his career, he ran nearly 20,000 head of sheep and a few thousand cattle on 50 miles of grazing land. Most of Laxalt's dogs were purchased, traded, or otherwise acquired from other shepherds or ranchers. These dogs were bred on ranches and in sheep camps to other Border Collies or Border Collie-type dogs. Today's Border Collies in America are descendants from the genetic pool of the early imports, as well as latter dogs imported in the early and mid-1900s from Scotland and England.

In the 1950s and early 1960s, the popularity of the Border Collie in the United States as a working dog began to really take off—much to the credit of Arthur Allen, who was the first to hold training clinics in the United States. He helped educate and train working Border Collie owners, traveled with Roy Rogers, and was the organizer

and director of the North American Sheepdog Society. His breeding program had a marked effect on the breed in the United States. His Border Collies appeared in two Walt Disney movies, *Border Collies in Action* and *Arizona Sheepdog*.

In 1955, the Border Collie was accepted into the Miscellaneous Class of the American Kennel Club, where it remained for nearly 40 years. The breed experienced a surge in popularity as a working sheepdog in the early 1990s. In 1995 the Border Collie was accepted into the Herding Group and given full AKC recognition, and the rest, as they say, is history.

The majority of modern-day Border Collies continues to possess the characteristic herding abilities, keen instinct, and great power over sheep. Highly skilled, they continue to be the premier working dog on farms, ranches, and in sheepdog trials. Some of the dogs are registered; others are not. As is typical of the Border Collie, they continue to vary in appearance, size, color, and markings.

THE CONTROVERSY: HERDING DOG VERSUS SHOW DOG

There's no getting around a look at the controversial relationship between working Border Collie owners and the American Kennel Club, a contemptuous and ongoing feud that makes the Hatfields and McCoys look like amateurs.

Border Collies are not new to AKC competitions. A member of the AKC's Miscellaneous Class since 1955, the breed has been allowed to participate in obedience and tracking trials with an Indefinite Listing Privilege number. This nearly 40-year arrangement suited the majority of Border Collie owners—especially obedience trainers who competed in AKC obedience trials.

In 1994, the AKC Board of Directors announced it was making

changes to the Miscellaneous Class and returning it to its original purpose as a short-term "holding" class for breeds seeking recognition. Obedience competitors began to worry because this meant they would no longer be able to compete in AKC-sanctioned obedience trials with their Border Collies. Working Border Collie owners, those who work their dogs on ranches and farms and compete in Border Collie trials, felt the AKC's sole purpose of moving the Border Collie into the Herding Group was to grant the breed full AKC recognition, thereby allowing it to participate in the AKC conformation ring.

How the Border Collie Got His Name

The name Border Collie has its origins with James A. Reid, a solicitor from Airdrie, Scotland and secretary of the International Sheep Dog Society from 1915 to 1948. For many years, working sheepdogs were referred to by shepherding folk as "Collies" and sometimes they still are, but the Kennel Club objected to the use of Collie, which they regarded as belonging to the Scots Collie (the Lassie-type dog). Two different breeds with the same name meant confusion, so James Reid agreed to use the term Border Collie for the sheepdog. While the time frame of all this is open for debate, most experts agree it was 1915.

Here's the controversy: like the forefathers of the breed, working Border Collie owners have had one primary concern—to safeguard the breed's supreme intelligence and herding instinct. They advocate herding instinct over physical appearance and oppose any written description or breed standard. They fought tooth and nail against AKC recognition, fearing that once the breed began to appear in the show ring, its herding ability would no longer be a primary focus. Border Collies would become "show" dogs, pets, and companions rather than superior workmates. They feared that AKC recognition would further increase the breed's popularity, and over time, the breed would be bred for looks, essentially splitting the Border Collie into two different breeds—a working breed and a show breed, perhaps not to the same extent, but not unlike the dichotomy in the early 1900s when the "show collie" eventually morphed into the Rough Collie. They also felt the AKC was using the Border Collie to pad its coffers and had no real interest in the future health and well-being of the breed..

On the flip side, proponents of full AKC recognition loved the breed equally, but they felt the breed had more to offer than simply herding ability. They wanted to pursue those avenues, which included the show ring. In their defense, they cited the fact that Border Collies have been shown in the breed rings in New Zealand for more than 60 years, in Australia for more than 30 years, and in Great Britain for nearly 20 years. They even modeled their breed standard after the show standards from Great Britain, Australia, and New Zealand.

The proverbial line in the sand was drawn, and opponents

and proponents took up their position, while others were caught in the middle. Rumors and accusations flew, egos were bruised, friendships were severed, and in the end, despite pressure to the contrary, the AKC Board of Directors voted for full recognition. In 1995 the Border Collie was admitted into the Herding Group, which included show classification in breed or bench shows, as well as participation in AKC herding, agility, tracking, and obedience events.

To this day, the feud between working Border Collie owners and those owners who choose to register their Border Collies with the AKC is still going strong with no end in sight.

Where to Register

- American Border Collie Association (ABCA)
- American Kennel Club (AKC)
- Canadian Border Collie Association (CBCA)
- International Sheep Dog Society (United Kingdom)
- Kennel Club in the UK
- North American Seep Dog Society
- United Kennel Club (UKC)

Will a "pretty" show dog lose his working instincts; does a top-notch working dog have to look good? These are questions today's Border Collie fanciers debate religiously.

CHARACTERISTICS
of the Border Collie

In most breeds, a breed standard is considered a good thing. It is a breeder's blueprint for success, and it describes the perfect dog to which they aspire and against which judges compare the dogs exhibited before them. To the newcomer, it may seem nothing more than a cluster of strange-sounding words strung together on a piece of paper. However, it is a detailed description of the *perfect* canine specimen, describing everything from height, weight, color and coat, to angulation of limbs, eye size, color, and shape, and what a dog should look like when he is moving.

However, the majority of working Border Collie owners—those who work their Border Collies on farms and ranches and compete in sheep dog trials—believe the breed standard is nothing more than a recipe for conformity, somewhat like trying to fit a square peg into a round hole. They oppose a breed standard, or written description of how the breed should look, for two reasons: 1) they don't particularly care what a Border Collie looks like physically. Their primary concern is not the dog's size, coat or eye color, or even his head shape (hence, the wide variations in Border Collie appearance). They believe a dog's skill and working ability should supersede all other requirements because at the end of the day, it all comes down to whether or not the dog can do his job and do it all day long, be it pushing stubborn sheep across a creek bed, through a gate, up steep mountain slopes, or into a dipping tank. These are the qualities valued by an owner who must get a day's work done, be it on the farm, ranch, or on a trial course; and 2) they feel that breeding Border Collies for physical characteristics rather than their skill in working livestock is detrimental to the breed's future.

That said, working Border Collie owners do care a great deal about structure because it is a critical and essential component when it comes to producing Border Collies who can perform the job for which they were originally bred. However, it is difficult to quantify or express the ideal working structure in a breed standard. This is not, as they say, a "cookie-cutter" breed. For example, a Border Collie who works in a feedlot or on a small farm may have a different structure than a Border Collie who works with sheep on the hills. He may not have (or need) the same well-laid back shoulder angulation or length of leg as his working counterpart. At the risk of sounding redundant, it all comes down to whether or not the dog can carry out the tasks for which he was originally bred and accomplish those tasks with the greatest amount of ease.

For more than 125 years the Border Collie has been selectively bred for a specific function—to work. Farmers, ranchers, and shepherds in the late1800s and early 1900s may or may not have cared diddly about 45-degree shoulder angulation or a 10:9 ratio of body length to height, but they had extensive knowledge of dogs in a working environment, and they had the uncanny ability to breed structurally sound dogs. Their livelihood depended upon doing so, and they did not need a breed standard to tell them how to do it. The proof, as they say, is in the pudding. If a dog did not work or structurally hold up over time, he was not used for breeding. On the other hand, dogs who excelled in a working environment had to be physically capable of doing the work for which they were bred. As a result, good working dogs were bred to other good working dogs, which naturally produced structurally sound dogs. The process is slightly more complicated, but the formula for producing working sheepdogs has held up for well over 125 years, and it is a formula

All Border Collies must have a sound structure, though their physical characteristics may differ depending on their specific task.

that suits today's working Border Collie owners just fine.

INTRODUCTION OF A STANDARD

When the Border Collie breed received AKC recognition, the Border Collie Society of America (BCSA), the breed's American Kennel Club parent club, was given the task of coming up with an acceptable AKC-breed standard they believe describes the ideal working Border Collie.

Working ability was the number one priority in the development of the Border Collie breed. Conformity

A standard helps perpetuate identifiable characteristics over generations so that a Border Collie maintains its difference from other breeds.

of type and appearance is a more modern requirement. So, with apologies to those Border Collie owners who are adamantly opposed to any type of breed standard or physical description, this section takes a closer look at exactly what a breed standard is, what it means, and what the different standards say.

In addition to the AKC breed standard, which is overseen by the BCSA, The Kennel Club in the United Kingdom oversees their own breed standard. Australia and New Zealand also have their own breed standards. The AKC standard was modeled after the show standards from England, Australia, and New Zealand, and with the exception of minor variations, the standards describe basically the same dog. The primary differences between the standards are the amount of detailed description and their phraseology.

Unlike some breed standards that were written more than 100 years ago and contain elegant yet old-fashioned words and terminology, the Border Collie standard is fairly simplistic and straight forward. However, to fully understand the picture of the ideal Border Collie, it is helpful to attend dog shows, herding trials and seminars, and, if possible, latch on to an experienced breeder, handler, judge or mentor and drive them crazy with questions.

BREED TYPE

When you see a Border Collie, you know he is a Border Collie without consciously stopping to think about it. But how? How do

you differentiate him from, say, an Australian Shepherd or a Bernese Mountain Dog? Is it the dog's color? Size? Self-assured presence? Is it the way his wedge-shaped head blends in proportionally with his body? One is not likely to confuse a Border Collie with a Cardigan Welsh Corgi even though both dogs were originally used as herding dogs. What separates one breed from another are the breeds' individual attributes and characteristics. These attributes and characteristics are called *breed type*—or in canine terminology, the *essence* of the breed. Breed type is a breed's complete package, including mental and physical characteristics that define what he is, how he looks, how he works, and his deportment—how he conducts himself. In herding breeds, a breed's working style—its method and manner of working livestock—also plays an important part in defining breed type.

Breed type is rooted in a breed's origin—the original purpose and function of a breed. The Border Collie has identifiable characteristics, such as color, markings, the dropped shoulder or crouch position, and the unmistakable Border Collie "eye" that were developed for a specific purpose and bred into the breed long enough that they have become stable, recognizable, and are reproduced with some uniformity. These individual attributes and characteristics are unique to the Border Collie breed. They are the distinguishing features that help identify a Border Collie.

Character and Temperament

One of the most important breed characteristics of the Border Collie—in addition to his herding instinct—is his character and temperament. Again, think back 125 years to the Border Collie's original purpose and function. He came from England's border country where farmers and shepherds needed a sturdy, hard-working dog who could flaunt his intellectual prowess and herding instinct while covering long distances and working in all conditions of weather. He needed to be sensitive enough to take direction from his master, yet intelligent enough to sense trouble, make snap decisions, think for himself, and operate without command because he often worked out of sight of his master. He needed stamina to travel great distances, sometimes as much as 10, 12 or 15 miles in a day, and to keep it up for hours on end. He needed exceptional athletic ability—to run as fast as the wind, switch directions without stopping, crouch, creep, circle, whip around or spring into immediate action if a group of sheep were to break off from the band. Equally important, he needed to love working with and for his master.

In his 1976 book, *A Shepherd Watches, A Shepherd Sings*, sheepherder Louis Irigaray captures the essence of character. "The dogs are workers, employees paid with an evening meal and a pat on the head, vital in every phase of a sheep operation. If the sheep are to be dipped in a hole in the ground, bathed in the chemical creosol to kill lice and ticks, five thousand of them headed for a hated swim, canine power sends them out of the corrals and into the tanks. There are no union problems and no other workers on earth are as anxious to get on with the job at hand."

A Border Collie's temperament and working ability go hand-in-hand. A dog who has a lot of working ability but an unsuitable temperament—for instance, an independent dog who has little use for human guidance or interaction—won't make a good working dog because he will have little or no desire to work as a team with his owner. If a dog is very nervous or worries a lot, it will override his ability to work. A very dominant sheep dog will always want to do things his way, which can try the patience of even the most experienced handler. On the other hand, a Border Collie can have the best temperament in the world, but if he has no herding instinct he will be of little help to the farmer. He may make a great obedience or agility dog, but he won't be able to find employment as a working sheepdog.

Temperament

The AKC breed standard describes his temperament as "being energetic, intelligent, keen, alert, and responsive. An intense worker of great tractability, it is affectionate towards friends but may be sensibly reserved towards strangers. When approached, the Border Collie should stand its ground. It should be alert and interested, never showing fear, dullness or resentment. Any tendencies toward viciousness, nervousness or shyness are very serious faults."

The Border Collie "Eye"

"Eye" is not always easily defined, but it is one of the most fascinating and defining characteristics of the Border Collie breed. Some describe *eye* as a style of concentration or an "intense gaze" that gives a Border Collie the power to control and move livestock. In his book, *The Farmer's Dog*, author John Holmes writes: "It is really far more an attitude of approach than anything connected with the dog's eyes."

Eye is an inherited characteristic, and many breed experts think it dates back to wolves and the way they would stalk their prey at that time. Man then developed that eye into something more useful, mostly in Border Collies. Some dogs know how to use their eye immediately. Others need to have it developed by working and practice.

The AKC standard describes the breed's working style as

The Border Collie is "intelligent, keen, alert, and responsive," with the temperament to work hard but remain tractable.

gathering and fetching the stock with wide sweeping outruns. The stock is then controlled with an intense gaze known as "eye," coupled with a stalking style of movement.

Border Collies, as well as all herding dogs, need a certain amount of eye to be an effective working dog. Otherwise, the dog has no real connection to the sheep. By the same token, too much eye creates its own set of problems. A strong-eyed dog uses his eye to control the sheep. This type of dog moves in with authority. He likes to take control of the sheep, keeping them neat and tidy. He never concedes an inch of ground. Nor will he want to flank—move around the sheep in response to the handler's commands—as easily as a loose-eyed dog. A very strong-eyed dog is referred to as "sticky" because he fixates his gaze on one particular sheep—oftentimes the first one he comes to. It's as if he becomes mesmerized or fixated on one sheep. A sticky dog lacks power because sheep usually don't fear him. The dog could be nose to nose with a stubborn ewe and she would stand her ground, continuing to eat grass.

A loose-eyed dog uses some eye, as well as his body and physical presence to control the stock. Unlike his strong-eyed counterpart, the loose-eyed dog doesn't care about keeping things neat and tidy. He is easier to move around the stock, and he is willing to be placed anywhere the handler asks.

In between the strong-eyed and loose-eyed dogs are the medium-eyed dogs. Most handlers like a dog who has a medium eye, but as with nearly everything pertaining to Border Collies, it's a matter of preference. The type of livestock being worked will also make a difference in how much eye a person will want in a dog. A dog with the proper balance of eye and power can move the sheep where they may not necessarily want to go. If needed, he will go to the nose of a stubborn ewe to let her know who is boss. The dog's gaze is saying, "You will move or I will make you move." This type of dog can also stand his ground with a gaze that clearly says, "Don't take another step!" when a stubborn ewe thinks she can intimidate him or chase him off. It is the ultimate battle of the minds between the livestock and the dog.

Power

Power and eye need to be in balance, but power is not about the physical strength, size, or structure of a Border Collie. Think of it as more of an intimidation factor—whether or not the sheep fear the dog. Sheep have a natural fear of dogs, and they show this fear by bolting. It is not unusual for bolting sheep to pile on top of each other—often suffocating in the process. Others will bolt off cliffs or head first into a fence, breaking their necks. Sheep also have the uncanny ability to know exactly which dogs to fear and which dogs will stand up to them, chase them, or bite them. They know which dogs have the power to make them move and which ones do not. Sheep can also recognize a new or fresh dog as soon as he appears in the distance.

Border Collies with a lot of power are often said to be "hard"—meaning they are very keen and can be difficult to slow up or control. They have the power to move a stubborn ewe across a creek or stream. They think they are more knowledgeable about sheep than their owner—and usually they are! As a result they do not always listen to direction. This type of dog can try the patience of even the most experienced and knowledgeable dog handler.

At the other end of the spectrum are "soft" dogs. This type of dog has little or no power to move any ewe, let alone a stubborn one. Very soft dogs are usually quite happy to allow sheep to drift toward the pen rather than move them.

The intense gaze of the Border Collie is referred to as its "eye."

In between the extremes of hard and soft dogs are the moderate dogs. They are softer than the hardest dogs, but not so soft that they do not have any power. They tend to be more considerate and more apt to listen and take direction from their owner.

Forequarters

A Border Collie's forequarters, hindquarters, and feet comprise the breed's all important running gear. His forequarters, the combined front assembly that includes the shoulder blade down to the toes and everything in between—humerus, radius, ulna, and feet—support nearly 70 percent of his entire body weight. The forequarters act like shock absorbers to help reduce the jar on a dog's legs when he stops or when the ground is very hard. A front that is structurally sound is essential for speed and the constant up-and-down motions required for farm work. Border Collies need to jump over and slide under fences and gates, and crawl under bushes and underbrush. They need to be able to get out of the way of a sheep or cow and turn on a dime. A good front is also essential for the unmistakable Border Collie "crouch" and creeping position that allows them to move the stock by intimidating them with their "eye." A good front assemblage is essential not only for the working Border Collie, but also for those competing in agility and obedience.

A dog who combines both eye and power is able to stand his ground with sheep to convince them to move in the right direction.

Hindquarters

The hindquarters comprise the rear assemblage and include everything from the pelvis down to the toes. A correct hindquarter assemblage provides a dog with maximum drive, lift, and power for propulsion.

The AKC standard calls for hindquarters that are *broad and muscular* with strong hocks—the joint on a dog's hind leg that corresponds to the human heel—that may be *either parallel or slightly turned in.* The majority of show dog owners prefer hocks that are parallel, both for efficiency and aesthetics. However, working Border Collie owners often prefer slightly turned-in hocks—also known as *cow-hocked* or hocks that *lay-in*—because this increases a dog's ability to push off when going sideways, and makes him a bit faster in the turns. An extremely cow-hocked dog would have legs that interfere with each other—regardless of what he was doing.

The Border Collie's forequarters and hindquarters must be proportional and compatible in order for a dog to function efficiently as a whole. If a dog's front or rear assembly is out of sync, it produces a variety of gaiting problems, which can include crabbing, overreaching, pacing, and so forth. A poorly assembled forequarter or hindquarter interferes with a dog's speed and power, cutting down on his efficiency and ability to do his job with the greatest amount of ease.

Feet

Strong, sound feet are essential for the working Border Collie. As a herding dog, he is required to cover long distances over varying terrains and in all conditions of weather. Stickers, burrs, and sharp stones would wreak havoc with thin pads in a very short time. In his book, *Sweet Promised Land*, Robert Laxalt recounts how his father, Dominique Laxalt, a shepherd during the early 1900s, wrapped his dogs' feet in burlap to keep them from bleeding. While the dogs were tough "with strong legs and feet like leather," the rocky Nevada hillsides were unforgiving, and even a man's boots would last less than two weeks.

The AKC standard calls for feet that are *compact, oval in shape; pads deep and strong.* The compact foot gives a Border Collie the greatest amount of strength and spring, allowing for maximum endurance and agility.

Through the Middle

To work efficiently, a Border Collie needs an athletic body and a flexible torso, which allows him to move gracefully, yet still be nimble, light on his feet, and change directions quickly with less chance of injury. He also needs a well-sprung (curved) rib cage for maximum exercise tolerance, performance, and superior stamina.

A dog's chest cavity contains and protects a number of important organs, including his heart and lungs. The "spring" of a rib cage is directly related to a dog's chest capacity. A Border Collie's rib cage, according to the AKC standard, is *moderately long with well-sprung ribs*. This allows plenty of room for a dog's heart and lungs to expand during exercise or strenuous work. It stands to reason that a flatter spring would put greater restrictions on the heart and lungs because there is less room in the dog's chest cavity for the heart and lungs to expand when he is breathing hard. At the other end of the spectrum, a "barrel chest", as seen in Bulldogs, is useless on a Border Collie because it is not flexible and it would not allow a working Border Collie to make quick turns or crawl or slide under fences and bushes. Can you imagine a Border Collie with a Bulldog-type chest trying to sail over fences, under gates, snake through weave poles or fly through agility tunnels?

Gait

Gait is a term used to describe a dog's movement, such as trot or gallop. Efficiency and endurance are paramount for a working Border Collie. He needs stamina to travel great distances and keep it up for hours on end. He needs exceptional athletic ability—to run as fast as the wind, switch directions instantly, and spring into immediate action if a stubborn ewe were to get out of line. Any wasted movement expends valuable energy and contributes to early fatigue.

To maximize both efficiency and endurance, a working Border

Collie uses a *moving crouch (stealth)* gait when he is working close up or in contact with sheep. When necessary, this gait can *easily convert to a balanced and free trot,* as described in the AKC standard. It is considered the most energy efficient gate for sustained travel. Border Collies also utilize a gallop during an outrun—when traveling long distances out and around the stock.

Size, Proportion, Substance

A Border Collie needs size to be able to outrun his stock. However, working Border Collie owners would never discount a dog with exceptional working ability simply because he did not conform to the "ideal" size as listed in a breed standard. If a dog can work stock, it does not matter to those owners whether the dog is 18 inches (46 cm) or 22 inches (56 cm) tall at the withers—the area at the base of a dog's neck and the peak of his shoulder blades.

With that in mind, when one thinks of a Border Collie, size is an important part of the Border Collie's established breed type. One does not, for instance, think of Border Collies as being the size of the low-set Welsh Corgis or the taller Belgian Tervurens.

When thinking in terms of size, it is important to keep in mind why the Border Collie was originally developed. The forefathers of the breed needed a dog that was sturdy, fast, and agile—not too *coarse* (large and clunky) or too *weedy* (small and fragile.) When it comes to Border Collies, moderation is important—you never want extremes either way.

The Border Collie is described in the AKC standard as a *medium-sized dog.* The height at the withers varies from 19 inches (48 cm) to 22 inches (56 cm) for males, and 18 inches (46 cm) to 21 inches (53 cm) for females. The UK standard describes the *ideal* height of a Border Collie as 21 inches (53 cm) for males with bitches being *slightly less.*

Proportion

The key component when discussing any aspect of the Border Collie, including size, height, and weight, is proportion. A Border Collie must be correctly proportioned. Some call it *balance* or *harmonious balance* or even *symmetry.* Regardless of the terminology, the Border Collie must be correctly proportioned. According to the AKC standard, the Border Collie should be *well-balanced* and of *athletic appearance, displaying style and agility in equal measure with*

"Coming and Going"

In the show ring, a dog's physical structure is evaluated at a trot while "coming and going"—going away from and coming back to the judge in a straight line—and also while trotting sideways to the judge.

The Border Collie's hindquarters provide the drive and propulsion the breed needs to cover ground. His feet need to withstand varying terrain and weather for long periods of time.

soundness and strength. Its hard, muscular body conveys the impression of effortless movement and endless endurance. The standard also calls for a length-to-height ratio of 10:9, meaning the dog should be slightly longer than taller. For example, if a dog had a body length of 20 inches (51 cm), he should stand 18 inches (46 cm) tall at the withers. The length-to-height ratio is what helps to give the dog his length of stride, which is necessary to cover the ground. It is worth noting that the standard does emphasize that overall *balance between height, length, weight and bone is crucial and is more important that any absolute measurement.*

With the acceptance of the Border Collie by the AKC, it is not unusual to see differences in the physical size and appearance of working Border Collies and Border Collies bred for the show ring. For example, working dogs can vary widely in their size and appearance, while show dogs tend to be more symmetrical. Working dogs can be rangier and less manicured. Show dogs tend to be squarer with shorter legs and heavier coats.

While neither the AKC or UK standards list specific weight requirements, the AKC standard says, *dogs must be presented in hard working condition. Excess body weight is not to be mistaken for muscle or substance.*

Generally speaking, working Border Collies tend to be slimmer and fitter than their show ring counterparts. Border Collies who are too heavy lose their maneuverability, agility, and endurance. Equally important, an overweight Border Collie is at risk for developing myriad health problems, which are discussed in subsequent chapters. Unfortunately, many show ring judges tend to like dogs with more weight on them.

Coat and Color

A Border Collie's coat is a true working dog coat. At the risk of sounding redundant, it is important to think about the breed's function as a herding dog in the harsh, wet, and cold climate of England's northernmost border region. To keep him warm and dry, a Border Collie's coat is double-layered—meaning he has a water-resistant outer coat and a shorter, dense, insulating undercoat. This type of coat is also referred to as *double-coated* or *two-ply* coat. The undercoat is designed to act as a protective layer against water and is capable of enduring all conditions of weather. It sheds out in the early summer as temperatures begin to rise, and it requires regular grooming to prevent matting and to allow a new undercoat to grow in during the late fall or early winter.

Rough and Smooth

The outer coat, or topcoat, comes in two coat types: rough and smooth—and, of course, anything in between. The term *rough coat* is a bit deceiving to newcomers because one expects the outer coat to be rough. Quite the contrary. A rough coat is medium in length, often silky, and can be either straight or wavy. Dogs can also have feathering on their forelegs, haunches, chest and underside, but the coat on their face, ears, feet, and front of their legs is smooth. These coats are often preferred for the show ring because when properly maintained and groomed they are undeniably beautiful. While show

dogs are frequently favored for their beautiful, full, heavy coats, a Border Collie should never be dripping with coat. An excessive amount of coat is not only a hazard but also inefficient for a working sheepdog. No farmer would want that type of coat on his Border Collies.

The *smooth-coated* Border Collie has short, close lying hair, which can be a bit coarser in texture than the rough coat variety. It is not unlike the coat of other smooth-coated breeds, such as Dalmatians or Bull Terriers. The AKC breed standard notes *neither coat type is preferred over the other.* While it is highly unlikely you will ever see a smooth-coated variety in the breed ring, this type of coat is relatively low-maintenance and much easier to maintain on a farm or in a working environment. There is less chance of debris, such as snow,

A Border Collie is a medium-sized dog, though a sound specimen is not faulted for being slightly larger or smaller than the standard.

mud, manure, stickers, burrs, and whatnot, collecting on a dog's belly and legs and between the pads on his feet—any of which can slow a dog down or even impede his movement. Stories have been told of dogs with too much coat getting entangled in bushes and underbrush. Can you imagine an exhausted shepherd sitting around the campfire grooming his Border Collies? Spending countless hours each night removing cockleburs, sandburs, seedpods, mud, manure, or feces? I think not.

In between the rough-coated and smooth-coated varieties lie "in-between" coat types. If, for instance, a rough-coated Border Collie were bred to a smooth-coated Border Collie—the puppies would have coats somewhere in between the parents. Some puppies would be considered smooth coated, while others would be considered rough-coated or moderate-rough coated. All are acceptable Border Collie coats.

A Coat of Many Colors

Working Border Collies are bred for intelligence and working ability, and as a result, there is a great deal of diversity in their appearance. The traditional and most common Border Collie colors are black (a good jet black!) and white. Early handlers and breeders often preferred black and white dogs, and it remains the most prevalent color in working Border Collies—but not for the reasons you might think. There is a popular notion that shepherds and ranchers preferred the black and white dogs because they were easier to see when working at a distance. As one Irish handler says about black dogs without white markings, "It's harder to see where they've got to."

"Pattern White"

White factored or pattern white are terms used to describe a dog that is primarily white all over with some black patterns— sometimes referred to in breeder jargon as black body splotches. Though the terms pattern white and body splotch are used frequently in canine terminology, they are neither scientific nor veterinary terms.

The truth is, dogs who excelled at working were used for breeding, and the dogs who excelled 100 years ago were mostly black and white dogs. As a result, black and white dogs were bred more often because only good working dogs were bred to other good working dogs, which, of course, produced more black and white dogs.

Another popular idea—and one favored by some handlers—is that a dog with the proper ratio of black and white has a calming effect on the stock. Totally black dogs, on the other hand, are great workers but are said to put too much pressure on the stock. White dogs are thought to lack presence with the stock, and as a result, the stock won't move for them. Some surmise it is because the sheep

This dog has a rough coat – it's of medium length and silky, with feathering on the legs and tummy.

have no fear of a dog of their own color.

That said, no serious working Border Collie breeder would ever breed for a specific color. They breed for working ability. As a result, black and white remains the most common color in today's Border Collies. However, the AKC and UK standards allow for a wide variety of colors, patterns, and marking, including *solid color, bi-color, tri-color, merle, and sable dogs.*

There are two colors in which the merle pattern may appear—the red merle and the blue merle. The red merle is a modification of the basic red body color, while the blue merle is a modification of the black body color. According to historians, the true blue merle comes from the old name "blue marled" or marbled. Merle patterns can range from extremely contrasting to evenly blended. Red merle and blue merle Border Collies are not very common in the United States. However, they are seen more frequently in Texas and the southern parts of the United States.

Other uncommon but perfectly acceptable Border Collie colors include sable, blue (or slate grey), tan, brindle, fawn (a dilution of liver), and lilac, which is known as *silver* in the Weimaraner, *Isabella* or *fawn* in the Doberman Pinscher, and *fawn* in the Australian Kelpie.

CHARACTERISTICS OF THE BORDER COLLIE

While Border Collies are a wellspring of affection and comfort, there are important mental and physical requirements associated

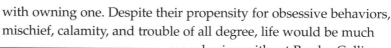

with owning one. Despite their propensity for obsessive behaviors, mischief, calamity, and trouble of all degree, life would be much more boring without Border Collies. Understanding why they do what they do will go a long way in building a happy, mutually respectful human/canine relationship.

Patterns and Markings

Border Collies can have many patterns and markings. Perhaps the most common is the half-white or split face. Rumor has it that hill shepherds may have purposely selected for this look. Here's the theory: If a hill shepherd was working two black dogs in the hills, both dogs would look basically the same. From a distance, it would be nearly impossible to tell one dog from the other. There is a popular notion that the hill shepherds began selecting for the half-white or split face in order to distinguish one dog from the other while they were far away. If one dog had a black face and the other had a half-white face, it would be much easier to tell them apart. It seems a logical explanation and it may in fact hold some truth, but as with many historical accounts pertaining to dogs, we may never really know for sure if it is fact or legend.

Personality Profile

The breed standard describes the ideal temperament of the Border Collie. In the real world, Border Collies can run the gamut in temperaments, and the genetic lottery can produce Border Collies who are good natured, mellow, shy, sulky, nervous, or fearful, as well as hyperactive or dog-aggressive. Some dogs are fantastic at working sheep but are fearful of humans. Others dislike children. Some are extremely noise sensitive. Almost all of them are high-octane, high-drive dogs who love to be included in every activity, be it biking, swimming, or riding in the car.

As a general rule, viciousness is not a problem in Border Collies. In most instances, viciousness is usually traceable to very bad handling or a hereditary defect. Most well-bred Border Collies acquired from reputable breeders possess the classic Border Collie temperament: high energy, super intelligent, sensitive, fast, gentle, sweet-natured, happy, and honest.

Defining Temperament

Generally speaking, the best indicator of a puppy's temperament is the disposition and activity level of the mother and father. If, for example, a puppy is a product of parents who both possess exceptional temperaments, there is a high probability that the puppy will inherit the same exceptional temperament and will show his parents' influence throughout his life. There are, of course, exceptions to the genetic lottery and some puppies, regardless of their parent's genetic contribution, grow into adult dogs with unstable temperaments. Environmental influences and conditions under which a puppy is whelped, reared, and socialized also play important parts in defining his temperament.

Most knowledgeable breeders can match the personality and temperament of a particular dog with the right family, which makes finding a knowledgeable and reputable breeder doubly important.

BORDER COLLIES AS PETS

The topic of Border Collies as pets has sparked spirited and heated debates among breed enthusiasts. Most working Border Collie owners dislike seeing the breed as a pet, feeling that Border Collies should remain working dogs. We regularly hear that Border Collies do not make good pets because they are bred for the specific function of herding, which requires intelligence, stamina, and gobs of energy. Border Collies have a type-A personality with a get-it-done-right-now attitude. They are high-octane pets who are not happy sitting around the house all day. They quickly become bored and destructive if they are not given the proper attention and exercise they need. Remember, Border Collies were and still are bred for longevity and staying power. They can work long hours and cover enormous distances in all conditions of weather. The working stiffs of the herding world, they can move 2,500 head of sheep across thousands of acres; push stubborn sheep across creek beds or up mountain slopes; and go to the nose of the most willful ewe. They have tireless endurance, often working all day with only an occasional break for rest. Even today, they can complete an 800 yard (720 meter) outrun in about a minute. So, a 10-minute stroll around the block does not come close to meeting the exercise requirements of a Border Collie in his prime.

Border Collies are their own reality show. A by-product of their herding instinct is their penchant for attacking moving objects including lawnmowers, weed-whackers, and vacuum cleaners. Others have been known to attack wheelbarrow tires, puncturing them with a single bite. Rakes, brooms, and snow shovels are equally stimulating

Though the standard allows for a variety of colors, black and white is the most common color combination.

to them. Some will gleefully shake cherished rugs, pillows, shoes, leather purses, and carelessly discarded undergarments into oblivion.

Because they are highly intelligent, highly complex creatures, it is not unusual for their obsessions to develop into obsessive-compulsive behaviors. Stories have been told of Border Collies who become mesmerized by reflective surfaces, such as mirrors, glass, or the stainless steel on refrigerators and dishwashers. Others go berserk at the sight of a fly. Some snap at the rain. More than a few Border Collies are mesmerized by the television or obsessed with sidewalk cracks. Others spin in endless circles. More than a few Border Collies have been surrendered to humane societies, abandoned, or given to rescue organizations because of their propensity to herd small children by biting and nipping at their ankles.

Therefore, it is understandable why many breeders and organizations do not recommend Border Collies as pets. However, the fact remains that each year thousands of Border Collies are placed in pet homes. If you take the time to understand the breed, and you are willing to spend a significant portion of your day exercising, training, and interacting with your Border Collie, you can end up with a wonderful pet and cherished companion.

The Key to Success

As with any breed of dog, the key to a happy and successful human-canine relationship is matching the right dog with the right owner. It is a fact that not all Border Collies will make good pets. There are some Border Collies whose work is their life. They eat, sleep, drink, and think of nothing else but working. They can be pushy and bossy, and they always think they are more knowledgeable about sheep than their owner—and usually are! Some of the best working dogs belong to this category, but it takes an experienced dog person to manage and bring out the best in them. This type of Border Collie is not a good pet dog. To put

Border Collies are high-energy dogs who want to be involved in all family activities.

him in the hands of an inexperienced dog person or to relegate him to the isolation of a backyard is the height of cruelty.

Border Collies can and do make great pets if you are committed to giving them the physical exercise and mental stimulation they need. There is no such thing as a part-time Border Collie! You will need to educate yourself about the breed and understand the time and energy requirements necessarily to live harmoniously with an extremely intelligent, high-drive, high-energy

Is the Border Collie, with its type-A personality, a suitable pet? That's another debate around this breed that has continued for ages.

dog. You will need to commit yourself to establishing a human-canine relationship that is built on a mutual foundation of love, respect, and trust. You must start obedience lessons right away and continue to reinforce the commands throughout his entire life.

First and foremost, the Border Collie is a working dog who needs a job. The job does not necessarily need to be herding, but you will be required to take up a variety of other sports, such as obedience, agility, flyball, flying disc, jogging, swimming, or hiking, in order to give your dog a job. Couch potatoes, workaholics, or full-time moms with a new baby might want to seriously consider, say, a Bulldog who is known for his low-energy lifestyle.

Successful Border Collie owners tend to have a high level of energy themselves. If you don't stay two steps ahead of your Border Collie at all times, he is likely to become stressed and develop obsessive-compulsive behaviors. You will need to be patient and firm, but not overbearing. You must love to spend the majority of your free time with your dog because your Border Collie will want to spend all of his time with you. Most important, you will need a sense of humor and a great deal of intestinal fortitude when things begin to go wrong. Once you've mastered all that, owning a Border Collie is nothing more than a full-time job.

Living Arrangements

In an ideal world, all Border Collies would live in the country with hundreds of acres of rolling hills and plenty of sheep to work all day, every day! In the real world, many working Border Collies

This Border Collie's zeal for playing with the sprinkler is characteristic of the abundance of energy the breed possesses.

live in a rural environment, but a large portion also live in suburbia and big cities. Some live on farms, some in condominiums. Generally speaking, Border Collies do not make great apartment dogs—unless, of course, you are home all day and prepared to devote time to multiple and extended outdoor excursions, say eight or ten times a day. Their working instinct, high energy levels, and physical and mental requirements can turn apartment living into a nightmare for both dog and owner (and landlord!)

Regardless of where you live, your Border Collie should live with you—never relegated to the isolation of a backyard or tethered on a chain. This is neither fair nor humane. As previously mentioned, this is not a breed that does well unattended. Border Collies need social interaction with their owners. Despite their size and abundance of energy, Border Collies can and do make excellent house dogs when they receive appropriate training.

You will also need a secure, fenced yard or kennel area for those times when your dog must be outside to relieve himself or left alone for short periods of time. The fencing should be at least six feet tall and must be equipped with secure latches or locks that intruders, curious children, or gifted Border Collies cannot open. It is prudent to locate the fenced area in a portion of the yard that is not accessible to passersby and the taunting behavior of malicious children. Teasing or tormenting a confined Border Collie can cause an otherwise well-tempered dog to become frustrated and aggressive in reaction to the abuse. It also creates behavioral problems including spinning, pacing, and excessive barking.

Regardless of whether you live in the city, suburbia, or the country, you should never allow your Border Collie to roam at will. Unsupervised dogs can wreak havoc on livestock, not to mention your neighbors' cherished vegetable or flower garden. Free-roaming Border Collies may be stolen, hit by a car, poisoned, shot by neighboring farmers and ranchers, or, at the very least, develop very bad habits. They can be injured or killed fighting with other animals or lost forever.

Exercise Needs

Like humans, dogs need plenty of exercise to maintain their good health. Exercise is vital for stimulating your Border Collie's respiratory and circulatory systems and building strong bones and muscles. Exercise will ward off obesity—keeping your Border Collie fit and lean. It nourishes and energizes a Border Collie's mind, keeping him active, healthy, and alert. Exercise and interactive play between a Border Collie and his owner can help eliminate loneliness, stress, and boredom, which are often the primary causes of unwanted behaviors including destructive chewing and chronic barking.

Owners who understand the needs of their Border Collies and give them positive outlets for their energy and drive are rewarded with an abundance of trust, faith, and love.

Exercise is a great way to give your Border Collie plenty of attention while building a strong human / canine relationship. Contrary to public opinion, most dogs will not run out in the backyard and exercise themselves—regardless of how big their fenced yard might be. Most generally, dogs will sit at the door—or chew and dig to entertain themselves—while they wait for their owners to come outside and join them.

Any exercise program needs to be tailored to suit your Border Collie—taking into account his age, health, and overall physical condition. A puppy, for instance, will tire more quickly than an adult Border Collie. Therefore, a puppy will require short but multiple exercise periods spaced throughout the day. You will also need to take plenty of care with your Border Collie puppy. He may act tough but his body is young and tender, and he can easily be injured when jumping, twisting, turning, or getting his body slammed by a bigger dog. Much will depend on your dog's overall physical and mental health and individual energy level. However, it is safe to say that a healthy adult Border Collie will require more than a brisk walk around the block to satisfy his energy requirements. Remember, they are built for endurance. They can run from sun-up to sun-down and still have energy to herd the kids, play flying disc, or retrieve a ball.

Mental exercise is as important as physical exercise. So you will need to come up with fun games that stimulate your Border Collie's brain. For example, teach him to wave, walk backwards, spin, twist, speak, jump through a hoop, or find a ball hidden in a box or under a bucket.

As with any exercise program, it is important to start slow and gradually work your way up to higher levels. Like most breeds, your Border Collie is susceptible to heat stroke, so it is best to confine your exercise and training to the cooler parts of the day. If you notice signs of fatigue, including heavy panting, you should allow your Border Collie plenty of time to rest and cool down. If your Border Collie is overweight, injured, or out of condition, it is prudent to consult with your veterinarian before beginning any exercise program.

Your Border Collie must get sufficient exercise to stay healthy physically and mentally.

Border Collies and Other Pets

With proper socialization and a good dose of common sense on the owner's part, most Border Collies can and do live happily with other animals, be they other dogs, cats, horses, goats, or llamas. Many Border Collies accompany their owners on trail rides and happily accept horses. Others live on farms and in rural environments with other animals—goats, pigs, chickens, and the like.

It is important that Border Collies be introduced to other animals in a safe, positive, and controlled environment—a controlled environment where owners are controlling the situation, not the dog! It is about management and expectations. What type of behaviors will you accept? How about chasing, harassing or bullying the cat, the goats, or other dogs? Hopefully not! You manage and control the situation so your puppy is not put in the position of being allowed to develop bad or fearful behaviors.

For instance, some inexperienced owners find it cute when their young puppy squares off with another dog. It is far from amusing when that same puppy grows into a strong, determined adult dog who challenges other dogs, is dog-aggressive, can't be taken out in public, and is eventually surrendered to the humane society or euthanized when he kills or maims another dog.

On the other hand, if other dogs bully your Border Collie puppy, he may grow into an adult dog who is afraid of other dogs. Many novice or inexperienced owners inadvertently allow their puppies to be bullied because they do not know what dog play looks like. Dogs run, chase, play bite, tug at body parts, yip, yap, body slam, and knock each other down. Most of the time, it is great fun for the dogs—provided both dogs are enjoying the game. So how do you tell when a fun game has turned into a rumble? It is important to watch both dogs body language—the dog chasing and the dog being chased. Are your dog's ears up? Is he returning the play? Or is your dog trying to literally run away? Is your dog nervous or frightened? Is he cowering? Is his tail between his legs? If so, the game has crossed the line into bullying, and you need to intervene.

Dog-aggression can also result when owners interfere in normal dog-to-dog interactions on neutral territory. Owners will tighten up on the leash when another dog approaches. This tells the dog, "Mom is worried. Something must be wrong. I'd better protect her from this other dog."

Generally speaking, dogs of the opposite sex are less likely to

Exercise Your Senior

Do not neglect your older Border Collie. A senior dog needs exercise to keep his body and systems functioning properly. The exercise, of course, will not be as strenuous as a younger dog's, but it should be regular exercise and enough to keep him active, alert, and healthy.

When properly introduced, Border Collies get along with most other animals, including donkeys and horses.

squabble or fight. Long before dogs were domesticated, they lived in packs and survival was based on a hierarchal system. Males fought other males mainly to establish their position in the group. Rather than fight to the death, the loser survived because that was in the best interest of maintaining the species. That's not so say male-to-male fighting doesn't wreak a lot of havoc and cause some serious damage until a human intervenes or the subordinate dog cries "Uncle." A female's aggression, however, stems from the instinct to protect her babies. Survival of the enemy was of no particular interest to her. For this reason, even today, fights amongst females generally have more severe consequences than encounters with males. They almost always require human intervention; otherwise they may fight to the death.

Border Collies and Children

If you navigated adolescence with a Border Collie, or any dog for that matter, no doubt you were loved unequivocally. Together you almost certainly passed the days running, jumping, and swimming. He probably tracked mud in the house, licked your face, rode shotgun in the family car, and nipped at your legs as you tore up the neighborhood on your bike. In retrospect, one might question how either of you (or your parents!) survived the chaos and litany of disasters. Border Collies still are the best and most delightful of childhood cohorts, but with guidance.

First and foremost, dog are pack animals. They have a clearly defined chain of command. They respect those members of the pack who are higher up in rank than they are, and they do not respect members of the pack who are lower. In a domesticated society the leader of the pack must always be you. Otherwise, dogs, like toddlers and teenagers, quickly learn which family members they can manipulate. As the pack leader, and a responsible dog owner, it is up to you to teach your puppy—and your children—which behaviors are acceptable and which are not. This will take a great deal of time and effort on your part, but it will allow your puppy to grow into a well-behaved adult dog capable of living in a domesticated society. Acquiring a Border Collie and then throwing the kids and the dog in the backyard with no supervision is a recipe for disaster. It's a safe bet that you will end up with a very unhappy child and a dog on the fast track to Border Collie rescue.

Furthermore, buying a puppy for your children and expecting them to look after his daily needs is a fantasy that exists only in the movies! In real life, it is never practical or realistic to expect a young child to assume all of the duties of rearing and caring for a dog, and more often than not, it is the dog who pays the price for your well-intended optimism.

Generally speaking, most good-natured Border Collies do quite well in a household when they are raised with children, established guidelines are followed, and children are clearly supervised. Border Collies may be tough enough to herd sheep in England's border country, but even the most accepting Border Collie may not tolerate the rough-and-tumble behavior of young kids who try to smother them with affection, tug on their ears or tails, bang pots on their heads, or poke little fingers in their eyes. These types of behaviors can startle, frighten, and even injure a Border Collie.

Teach Your Children Well

Parents are the key figures when it comes to teaching children how to interact safely with a dog: how to pet him, feed him, hug him, talk to him, and play with him. From day one, it is important that you teach your child some basic, common courtesies just as you would with other family members. For instance, you would not allow a child to jump on a parent or sibling who is sleeping, or barge into a bathroom without knocking. The same considerations apply to the family dog, such as teaching children not to disturb him when he is sleeping, eating, or chewing a bone.

What Children Should Learn About Dogs

Children who are raised with dogs need to understand that not all dogs are as lovable and well behaved as their own Border Collie. Children should learn:

- To ask permission before petting a strange dog.

- To offer their hand with their palm facing up (like feeding sugar cubes to a horse). Some dogs hate to be patted on the head and will shy away or possibly nip.

- To never go into a house or yard where a dog is present unless the owners are in attendance.

- Stay away from chained, fenced, or stray dogs.

- Always get help from an adult when dealing with an injured dog, as they are more likely to bite as a reflex to the pain.

- Never stare directly at a dog. The dog may perceive this as a challenge.

Border Collies of all ages can make wonderful life-long companions for children who also understand the dog's characteristics and needs.

Young children, generally under the age of seven, do not understand the consequences of their actions. They see nothing wrong with trying to pick up a puppy by his ears or by wrapping their arms around his neck and squeezing with all their might. They do not understand they can seriously injure a puppy or young dog if they pick him up incorrectly or, heaven forbid, drop him. Equally important, dogs can't say, "Leave me alone, I'm eating" or "Don't pull on my tail." They communicate by fleeing the area, growling, or biting.

On the other end of the spectrum, when a puppy is allowed to play unsupervised throughout his puppyhood with several young children, you end up with an adult dog that has learned to chase, jump, and nip at arms and legs in motion. Motion stimulates a puppy's natural instinct to chase and nip, and left unchecked, your puppy will see no harm in continuing this "game" when he is a 45-pound (20 kilogram) adult dog.

Equally important, Border Collies are attracted to the noise of moving objects. Remember the lawnmower, weed cutter, and vacuum cleaner? Children who run and scream while playing are as good as sheep in a pasture to the Border Collie. It is the Border Collie's nature to control his flock—to prevent them from escaping, and to bring back to the group any sheep that has strayed. The behavior of nipping and biting at the children's ankles is not an aggressive act, but rather an instinctual behavior that has been genetically programmed for hundreds of years. In the dog's eyes, the children (his flock of sheep) are getting away, and he is simply trying to control them. It is important that you understand and recognize this type of behavior so you can nip it in the bud immediately.

Border Collies also weigh quite a bit more than toddlers and small children. For no other reason, you should train your dog early on that jumping on people is never allowed. If you own a Border Collie, it is highly unlikely your children will survive adolescence without being knocked down a time or two. A 50-pound (23 kilogram) Border Collie on the move can easily—albeit accidentally—knock over a child with a simple bump.

Equally important, infants, babies, and young children should never, ever, ever under any circumstances be left alone with a dog regardless of how trustworthy your Border Collie may be. No dog is completely predictable with children. A dog may misread the strange sounds of an infant or the unpredictable behaviors of a toddler.

Children who learn to tend to the needs of their dog can learn responsibility, respect, and compassion. They learn that he will need water when he is thirsty, food when he is hungry, a bath when he is dirty, and peace and quiet when he is sleeping. At what age you begin teaching these responsibilities varies depending on the individual child. There are some things you can teach a four-year-old child but not a three year old. A child's individual maturity level as he gets older will dictate how much responsibility to give him in any part of life, including the responsibility of feeding and caring for a dog.

A puppy's cuteness often overrides our good sensibilities. Choosing a puppy based solely on looks is never a good idea. You must also consider his temperament, and a good breeder will help you choose a Border Collie that suits your family and lifestyle.

The Finer Points of Play

Play is a wonderful releaser of excess energy for both dogs and kids. They run, jump, swim, and go for bike rides. Children also need to be taught what games are and are not acceptable when playing with dogs. To prevent the situation from getting out of control, parents should always monitor and control the play between dogs and kids; play should be appropriate to the size and age of the dog as well as the child; think active rather than rough—avoid games that encourage or allow a dog to use his teeth, such as sic 'em or attack or wrestling games where a dog can become overexcited and inadvertently learn to use his teeth. Children should never be allowed to hit, kick, pinch, punch, bite, or harass a dog in the name of play.

PREPARING

Your Border Collie

wning a dog is an enormous responsibility. Owning a highly intelligent, incredibly active, and exceptionally intense breed that no doubt has at least one obsessive-compulsive behavior carries an added responsibility. There is no denying that Border Collie puppies are irresistible, magical, and charming with their cuddly good looks and puppy antics. While the majority of them can grow into sensitive, loving, caring companions, acquiring a Border Collie, or any dog, on impulse is a bad idea. A well-bred and well-cared for Border Collie can live to be thirteen, fourteen, or fifteen years of age. Caring for any breed of dog is a lot of hard work because he cannot take care of himself. Owning a Border Collie carries additional requirements because owners must possess an endless reserve of patience and energy, coupled with a dash of enterprising madness. More importantly, owning a Border Collie requires an exceptional owner who understands the physical and mental requirements of the breed and can remain two steps ahead of these intelligent creatures at all times.

For the next ten years or more, your Border Collie will depend on you for his food, water, shelter, exercise, grooming, training, affection, and regular veterinary care. He will look to you for companionship at all hours of the day. He will want to play when you want to relax. He will try to herd the kids, the cats, other dogs, horses, and even the vacuum cleaner. It is highly likely he will occasionally track mud through the house, refuse to come when he is called, and embarrass you in front of your friends, neighbors, and in-laws.

The good news is you need not go to the borderlands between England and Scotland to find the perfect Border Collie! Finding the perfect canine companion does, however, require time, intestinal fortitude, and a bit of detective work. You will need to do your homework and check on resources, familiarize yourself with the Border Collie breed, and research breeders. Sadly, there are some people breeding Border Collies purely for money with little interest in the future welfare of the dog. Therefore, you must talk to multiple Border Collie breeders, as well as trainers, veterinarians, and other Border Collie owners. You will need to separate opinion from fact,

Hopefully you spoke to multiple owners of Border Collies before deciding this was the right breed for you. If so, you'll be rewarded in spades.

which can be a daunting task for the newcomer.

BEFORE YOU DECIDE: DO YOUR RESEARCH

You should read, observe, study, and learn everything about the breed before purchasing a Border Collie. You must understand the Border Collie temperament so you can choose a dog that suits your temperament, lifestyle, and living conditions. If you and your Border Collie have different temperaments—if, for instance, you are mellow and he is energetic, or he is very independent and strong-willed and you are timid or reserved—life will be harder for both of you. Compatible temperaments can mean the difference between a happy partnership that lasts twelve or more years and a constant battle of wills, which may make you wish you had gotten a cat.

If you educate yourself and make wise choices in the beginning, you greatly increase your odds of having a long, happy, and rewarding relationship with your Border Collie.

PUPPY OR ADULT?

Acquiring a Border Collie puppy, as opposed to an older dog, allows you to start with a clean slate, so to speak. The puppy has no bad habits (yet!), and you can maximize his potential by molding his character, fostering his zany personality, and instilling all of the behaviors he will need to function as he grows bigger and bolder. You can set your own expectations and manage your puppy so he grows into a well-rounded, well-behaved adult dog.

The flip side is that raising a puppy is a lot of work. There is a reason puppies are cute and adorable; if they weren't…who in their right mind would spend 24-hours a day at their beck and call--feeding, pottying, and cleaning up after them? Unfortunately, that's why a lot of Border Collies end up in humane societies and rescue groups because when the "cuteness" wears off, they are still dogs that need to be trained, groomed, fed, exercised, and loved on a daily basis.

Raising a puppy is a lot like raising a human baby. Both are demanding, and they require a lot of time and energy—at all hours of the day and usually in the middle of the night. Puppies left to their own devices get into all kinds of mischief—barking, chewing, digging, and peeing on the rug.

The key is managing your puppy's environment 24-hours a day so he does not chew anything and everything in sight, pee from one end of the house to the other, or run into the street and get hit by a car. A puppy needs to be housetrained and obedience trained. He needs guidance and direction so he doesn't bark all night, chase other animals, or dig holes in your newly planted rose garden.

A Border Collie puppy requires an enormous amount of socialization. This is essential if you plan to raise a well-behaved, non-aggressive adult Border Collie. You need to invest time taking him to puppy socialization classes, walks in the park, and rides in the car. You will need to expose him to every possible situation he is likely to encounter as an adult, such as kids on bicycles, joggers, women in floppy hats, other animals, trashcans, and people in wheel chairs. Raising a puppy is a rewarding and life-changing experience but a lot of work! Don't let anyone tell you otherwise.

Adult Dogs

Puppies are cute, but there is a lot to be said for a well-trained adult dog. When you acquire an older Border Collie, say one, two or three years old, what you see is what you get. An older dog's personality is already developed, and his herding instinct, drive, and energy level are well established. With close observation, interaction, and help from a knowledgeable dog person, you should be able to determine the quality of his disposition and whether or not he will suit your personality and daily life. Is he timid? Aggressive? Bold? Is he energetic? Happy? Is he spoiled rotten? Does he get along with kids? Other animals?

Adult Border Collies become available for a variety of reasons. Many breeders, for instance, have one-or two-year-old herding, obedience, agility, or show prospects that did not pan out for a variety of reasons, but would make exceptional pets in the right home. Occasionally, adult dogs are returned to the breeder because the owner moved or is no longer able to keep the dog. Many of these dogs are well-bred and have been well cared for yet, for one reason or another, need to be placed in a good home.

Border Collie puppies are adorable, it's true, but they are not plush toys. They require a great deal of care.

Adult Border Collies can make wonderful pets, and are often at least partially trained.

Border Collies often are advertised "Free to Good Home" in local papers, which is code for "The dog has a lot of bad habits, he's driving me crazy, and I don't want him anymore." These dogs are often lacking in direction, management, and love, and have been allowed to develop annoying habits. In the right hands, they can make wonderful pets, but go in with your eyes wide open.

Purchasing an adult dog is not without risk, either. A show dog who has been raised in a kennel situation will most likely be crate trained, accustomed to traveling, and oblivious to the pandemonium of shows, but he may not be housetrained. A working Border Collie may be too energetic or intense, or he may have developed quirks or obsessive compulsive behaviors that are difficult if not impossible for the inexperienced owner to manage. Some Border Collies may not have been raised around kids, and they may or may not like kids. Some children are more active and vocal than others and this can annoy even the most stable dog. If you have children, most reputable breeders will want to meet them and observe how they behave and interact around dogs, and vice versa. Absent any problems, most kids and Border Collies that are properly introduced and supervised can develop a strong and loving relationship that will last a lifetime.

FINDING THE BORDER COLLIE OF YOUR DREAMS

Finding a Border Collie who suits your personality and lifestyle requires time, intestinal fortitude, and a bit of detective work. The good news is you need not go to the Borderlands to find your perfect Border Collie. Plenty of good Border Collies can be found almost anywhere in the country. You must, however, do your homework and check on resources, familiarize yourself with the Border Collie breed, and research the best places to find your dog. Sadly, some people breed Border Collies purely for money with little interest in the future welfare of the dog. Therefore, you should talk to trainers, veterinarians, and other Border Collie owners. You must separate opinion from fact, which can be a daunting task for the newcomer.

Knowledge Counts

Breeding purebred dogs is a labor of love, as well as an art and a science. Experienced Border Collie people are usually dog savvy, conscientious, and care about the welfare of their dogs, and dogs in general. They study pedigrees, plan litters, and breed only to maintain or improve the quality of the Border Collie breed. They recognize that each breeding must be undertaken with great care and forethought. Breeding stock is tested for genetic problems including hip dysplasia and collie eye anomaly, and only those dogs who are proven clear of problems are used for breeding purposes. Puppies are regularly and affectionately socialized to everything they are likely to encounter as adult dogs. Puppy aptitude tests, or some form of evaluation, are performed in order to assess a puppy's training requirements, competitive potential, and placement options.

Experienced Border Collie people can answer questions regarding the training, grooming, feeding, and handling of Border Collies, and dogs in general. Potential owners are screened, and dogs are sold only to those people who meet the qualifications necessary to provide a permanent, first-class home.

Purchasing a Border Collie from someone who understands and cares about the breed goes well beyond the sales transaction because that person will be there to help you through the transition periods, offer training advice, and help you make serious decisions regarding the care and well being of your Border Collie. If, for some reason, your particular Border Collie does not work out, they are often in a position to either take back the dog, help place it, or offer an appropriate solution.

In your search, it is highly likely you will come across people who are not interested in the betterment of Border Collies. People who breed dogs with little regard or concern for their dogs' ancestral background, working ability, or the finer points of the Border Collie breed. They are not necessarily bad people, and they do not always have bad intentions. Some of them truly love their dogs and provide

Male or Female?

When all is said and done, choosing a male or female dog usually comes down to personal preference. Some people are attracted to the masculinity of the males. Others love the femininity and slight refinement of the females. Generally speaking, females tend to mature physically a bit earlier than males. As a result, females might be more serious or emotionally more mature at a younger age. However, both males and females can make sweet, loving companions, and the pros and cons of either sex seem to balance each other out. When it comes to choosing a Border Collie, knowledgeable breeders know the capabilities of both sexes and are your best bet when it comes to assessing whether a male or female best suits your temperament, personality, and lifestyle.

good care. However, most are unaware they are contributing to an even larger problem—pet overpopulation.

These "backyard breeders" seldom have knowledge of pedigrees, genetic disorders, or the importance of socializing puppies. Normally, they are not involved in the sport of dogs, nor do they invest the time, money, or energy into producing dogs of sound health and temperament. Their breeding stock is generally not breed quality, meaning it does not meet or exceed the requirements necessary for producing healthy, sound, intelligent, working dogs. Puppies are generally sold on a first-come, first-serve basis with little regard for the future welfare or living conditions of the dogs. The dogs are seldom socialized properly, and a backyard breeder is likely to be of no future help to a puppy buyer if and when things begin to go wrong. They often wash their hands of the dog the minute he's been sold.

Purchasing a Border Collie from this type of person is a gamble. You may pay less up front for a dog, but it is highly likely that you will pay a good deal more in vet bills—especially if the dog has serious health or temperament problems.

Border Collies are pretty popular, but finding the Border Collie who is right for you will take some time and plenty of investigating. Puppies can be purchased and shipped long distance, be it across the state or across the country. However, unless you personally know the source has outstanding references, it is always a good idea to meet the puppy first. This allows you to view the facility and see all of the dogs. Selling dogs online has become increasingly popular. Unfortunately, not all breeders of Border Collies are reputable, and the dog you purchase online may be a far cry from what arrives at your doorstep.

Where to Begin Your Search

Breed clubs and registries, such as the American Border Collie Association (ABCA), the United States Border Collie Club (USBCC), the Border Collie Society of America (BCSA), the American Kennel Club (AKC), and the Kennel Club (KC), are good places to start. They can refer you to experts, provide information on the history of the breed, characteristics, and so forth.

Veterinarians are usually familiar with Border Collie people, the health of their dogs, and the level of care they provide to their dogs. They can usually provide you with a list of local people who are involved in the sport of dogs, Border Collies in particular.

Herding trials and dog shows are a must-do when searching for a Border Collie. They are great fact-finding missions because the best indicator of a puppy's temperament is the sire and dam. You can compare the quality of many Border Collies under one roof; talk to owners and handlers; see how they interact with their dogs; and watch dogs compete in different venues including herding, obedience, agility, and conformation. You can find information about dog shows from Infodog.com, local clubs, or national registries.

Questions to Ask Before Committing

It is important that you educate yourself about the Border Collie breed in general before beginning your search or, heaven forbid,

committing to a Border Collie. A basic understanding of the breed's temperament, genetic diseases, exercise requirements, and so forth, will allow you to ask informed questions. Experienced dog people are a valuable source of information, but separating them from the novice or inexperienced breeder can be a challenge if you don't know what you need to know. At the minimum, you will want to know:

- How long have they been involved with Border Collies? Look for someone who has longevity in the breed.
- Are the dogs registered? (This alone does not guarantee quality.)
- Do they belong to any local or national clubs / organizations?
- Do they compete in canine sports, such as herding, obedience, agility, tracking?
- What have they accomplished with their dogs? What titles have they earned?
- Will they supply a three-generation pedigree and/or health certificate?
- Are they willing to take the dog back if things do not work out?

Remember when making your choice that anyone can breed cute pups; only those with experience will help you understand what to expect from the breed.

Quick Tip

It is important to keep in mind that most, if not all, of the people you will be talking to are biased in their opinions. Of course they will tell you their puppies are the best! Try talking to as many people and visiting as many kennels as possible before making your choice.

Will they provide a full or partial refund?
- Will they be available if problems arise?
- Have the puppies eyes been examined by a canine ophthalmologist? Have they been dewormed? Vaccinated? And will the breeder supply copies of this documentation?
- Have the sire and dam been tested for genetic problems (i.e., hip dysplasia, cataracts) Will they supply you with copies of this documentation?
- How many litters do they breed yearly? Most responsible breeders produce one, two, or maybe three litters a year. Anything more may indicate a less than reputable outlet.
- Do they have references?

What They Will Want to Know About You

Most people involved in purebred dogs are passionate about dogs. They go to great lengths to place their dogs in the best possible homes. They will want to know about you, your family, and the environment in which the Border Collie will be raised. This information helps them to match the right dog with the right owners. For instance, a family with three or four energetic kids who like to swim, hike, and ride bikes may need a puppy with a different personality than someone looking for a ranch or herding prospect. Therefore, you should be prepared—and not offended—when you encounter dog people who are more tenacious than IRS auditors. A sampling of the many questions a breeder is likely to ask include:
- What is your knowledge of the Border Collie breed—and dogs in general?
- Why do you want a Border Collie?
- Have you ever trained a dog before? What breed?
- Do you currently own a Border Collie or any other breed of dog? Or other animals including cats, horses, goats?
- What happened to your previous dog? Did he happily grow old? Was he released to a shelter? Killed by a car? Did he escape your yard, never to be seen again?
- Will this dog be an indoor dog? Outdoor dog? Or a combination of the two?
- Do you have children? How many—and their ages?
- Are you active and energetic? Are you a workaholic who clocks 12-hour days?
- Are you assertive? Gregarious? Outgoing? Calm? Quiet? Timid?

Overbearing?

- Do you live in a house? Apartment? The city? Country? Do you rent or own a home?
- Is your yard fenced?

Rescue Organizations

Rescuing a purebred Border Collie is a viable option for many prospective owners. Border Collie rescue volunteers work tirelessly to educate the public, as well as rehabilitate and place purebred Border Collies in loving, permanent homes. Many wonderful, sensitive, and loving Border Collies are surrendered to rescue organizations because their owners did not understand the work and effort required in owning, training, and living with a herding dog. A significant number of owners did not understand nor were they prepared to deal with the compulsive or behavior problems that result when intelligent, high-energy dogs do not have acceptable physical and mental outlets for their energy. Behavior problems that can include destructive chewing, digging, chronic barking, or aggression toward other dogs.

Countless Border Collies are given away or abandoned because of their owners' ignorance, indifference, or lack of compassion. Many Border Collies are given up or abandoned after they outgrow the "cute stage." Some Border Collies in rescue have been abused or mishandled. Many lack proper socialization skills. Others have been accidentally lost or voluntarily relinquished to animal shelters or rescue groups by their owner or their owners' family because of personal illness, death, or other changes in circumstances. Pregnant bitches or young puppies occasionally find their way into rescue, but the majority of Border Collies are older dogs, over one year of age.

If you're interested in a working dog, watch the parents at work, if possible, and speak to breeders at length about what you want to do with your Border Collie. That way the odds will be on your side when you finally find your dog.

All Border Collies in rescue are evaluated carefully via temperament testing and then placed in experienced foster homes where they receive veterinary attention, obedience training, socialization, grooming, and loads of TLC until they can be placed in a permanent, loving home. Countless stories have been told of Border Collies once labelled "difficult" or "untrainable" who went on to excel in canine events such as obedience, flyball, herding, and agility, proving that dogs can flourish in the hands of responsible owners who know and understand Border Collies.

Purebred Border Collies who are adopted from rescue organizations are eligible to apply for an Indefinite Listing Privilege (ILP), which allows the owners of rescued purebreds to participate in AKC companion events including obedience, agility, and tracking.

Shelters

Border Collies of all ages find their way into humane societies for any number of reasons. Some are surrendered or abandoned by their owners. Others living in abusive conditions are confiscated by animal control officers and turned over to shelters. Lost or stray Border Collies are often taken to a shelter by caring and compassionate residents. Many of these dogs are young to middle-aged. However, it is not unusual for older Border Collies, some seven, eight, or nine years old, to end up in an animal shelter. Shelter personnel screen all Border Collies for temperament and placement before they become eligible for adoption. Many shelter dogs facing euthanasia are rescued by Border Collie rescue organizations and placed in foster homes for further adoption.

Many humane societies are now working with pet stores to find homes for shelter pets through in-store adoption centers. While many animal shelters are now state of the art, some owners continue to perceive them in a negative light. As a result, they refuse to set foot in an animal shelter or humane society. In-store adoption facilities provide local humane societies greater exposure and a popular and positive venue in which to educate owners, answer questions, and provide basic adoption services. In return, owners are exposed to and encouraged to interact with homeless dogs who might otherwise go unnoticed in a shelter environment. Equally important, it allows pet stores to give back to the community.

PREPARING YOUR HOME

Once you have made your selection, be it male or female, puppy or adult—fasten your seatbelt and be prepared for the time of your life!

To make the transition as smooth as possible, there are certain things you should do before bringing your new Border Collie home. Much of this information is geared toward preparing your home for a new puppy but applies equally to an adult dog. It is worth mentioning that when you obtain an adult dog whose background and training are a bit sketchy, such as a rescue dog, it is always a good idea to assume the dog has no training and begin his training as if he were a puppy.

Puppy Proofing

It is best to puppy-proof your house *before* your four-legged friend arrives. This includes anything your puppy is likely to seek out and destroy. Like toddlers, puppies will want to explore their surroundings and will try to put everything in their mouth—whether it fits or not. Your puppy is too young to understand that your expensive Italian loafers are not for teething. Pick up shoes, books, magazines, and pillows. Put up any houseplants, prescription bottles, waste baskets, and candy dishes. Tuck electrical cords behind furniture, under rugs, or tape them to the baseboards. Many objects, if swallowed, such as shoelaces, buttons, socks, marbles, paper clips, and disembowelled dolls, can cause life threatening intestinal blockage and maybe require surgery to remove.

You must also puppy-proof your yard, garden, and outdoor areas. This includes putting away anything your puppy is likely to consume including hoses, sprinklers, lawn ornaments, and poisonous plants such as azaleas, begonias, hydrangeas, and poinsettias. Be sure to store containers of poisonous products—antifreeze, fertilizers, herbicides, and the like—on shelves and out of reach from inquisitive, thrill-seeking Border Collies.

Older dogs with lots still to give are available through Border Collie rescue organizations across the country and around the world.

Some Border Collies are master escape artists, so make sure there are no holes in your fencing or broken gates that he is likely to escape through. If your property is not fenced, be sure your puppy is leashed each and every time he goes outdoors. He does not have the mental wherewithal to understand that the street is a dangerous place to be. It is your job to keep him safe.

DOGGIE ESSENTIALS

You will need basic doggie essentials including a leash, collar, food, food and water bowls, crate, dog bed, ID tag, and an assortment of training toys and chew toys.

Beds

Your Border Collie puppy will need a bed of his own, but it is best to hold off on the ultra deluxe designer model until he is well through the chewing stage. A tenacious chewer can turn a posh canine bed into worthless confetti in the few minutes it takes you to answer the telephone. A large blanket or towel folded over several times or a cozy fleece pad placed in his crate or exercise pen will do the job for the first few months. They are easily cleaned in the washing machine and therefore less likely to develop that distinctive doggie smell.

Asking questions and doing research will help you find the border Collie of your dreams.

Collars

There are countless types and styles of collar from which to choose, and they are generally made of leather, nylon, cotton, or hemp. They also come in a variety of styles: buckle, harness, head halter, half-check, greyhound, choke chain, and martingale.

Every Border Collie should wear a flat, lightweight nylon or leather buckle collar with proper identification attached. This is his ticket home should he become lost or separated from you. Nylon collars work well with puppies because you will need to replace them several times before they are fully grown. Nylon collars are relatively inexpensive and available at retail pet stores.

Leather collars are more expensive than nylon but well worth the investment for adult dogs, as they are softer yet sturdier, and given the right care they will last a lifetime. There are significant differences in the quality of leather collars, so if this is your preference, be sure to select a high-quality leather collar from a reputable manufacturer. Like fine wine and good cheese, high-quality leather gets better with time. Top-quality leather smells good, and it feels good in your hands, too. It's beautiful, soft, pliable, easy to grip, yet extremely durable.

Collar Styles

Several types of collars work by putting pressure on your dog's neck and throat, like choke chains and prong collars. While it may be tempting to use these devices on an energetic and intense dog like a Border Collie, these collars are best left to professionals. In the hands of an inexperienced person, these types of collars can cause serious damage to a dog's throat. Taking the time to train your dog to walk properly and not pull without these devices will be much more rewarding to you both.

If you have a Border Collie who is a nuisance puller for whom your best training efforts have not succeeded, you might consider a head halter—depending on your level of patience. A head halter goes over your dog's face and applies pressure to the back of the neck rather than the front of the throat. While they can be very effective, most dogs are not used to this type of configuration and it can require a great deal of preconditioning, patience, and diligence in order to make it a positive experience for your Border Collie.

Some owners choose a harness for their dog. Keep in mind, a harness will not keep your Border Collie from pulling, but it will take the pressure off his trachea. There are a variety of models available in different shapes, sizes, and materials. It is best to seek professional advice in order to correctly fit your Border Collie with a harness and prevent chafing.

Crates

If you own a Border Collie, a crate is an absolute necessity. Crates come in different shapes, sizes, and materials that offer their own advantages. Some are folding wire crates that provide good air circulation and help keep dogs cool when temperatures begin to rise. A variety of crate covers turn any wire crate into a secure den and provide protection from the elements. Other crate types include

The Right Fit

A buckle collar should be neither too tight nor too loose. Ideally, it should fit around your dog's neck with enough room to fit two fingers between his neck and the collar. It should not be so tight as to restrict his breathing or cause coughing, nor should it be so loose that it slips over his head. When too loose, the collar can easily snag on objects, such as shrubbery, a fence post or another dog's tooth or paw, causing the dog to panic and inadvertently hang himself. Equally important, growing puppies quickly outgrow their collars. Be sure to check the collar size frequently on puppies. Left unchecked, a collar can become imbedded in a dog's neck, causing serious health issues. Check your dog's collar regularly to ensure it is not frayed or worn.

heavy-duty, high-impact plastic kennels that meet domestic and international requirements for airline travel. An especially handy crate of this type is the Nylabone Fold-Away Carrier and Den, which has the added value and convenience of being easy to fold and store away when not in use.

There are also a variety of soft canvas and water-resistant-type crates that are ideal for home and travel. They are easy to set up and take down, and as an added bonus, are often machine washable. Some come equipped with extra features, such as zippered sides, storage pockets, carry bags, and wheels.

When shopping for a crate, you will want to purchase one that is big enough for your Border Collie when he is full grown. Ideally, it should be big enough for your adult Border Collie to stand up, turn around, and stretch out while lying down. If the crate is too big, it defeats the purpose of providing the security of a den. If it is too small, your Border Collie will be cramped and uncomfortable, and this is neither fair nor humane. During the housetraining stage, a crate that is too large allows a puppy to use one end for sleeping and the other end as a bathroom, which defeats the crate's usefulness as a housetraining tool. Some crates come equipped with a divider panel that allows you to adjust the crate space accordingly. This option allows you to block off a portion of the crate for housetraining purposes, and can take your Border Collie from the puppy stage through housetraining and into adulthood without the expense of purchasing multiple size crates. A good quality crate will last a lifetime, and the benefits definitely make it well worth the cost when one considers the alternative of replacing damaged carpet and furniture six months down the road.

When in doubt, ask a breeder, veterinarian, or knowledgeable dog person to recommend a size and style.

Exercise Pen

Like a crate, an exercise pen is indispensable for raising a well-behaved puppy. They are ideal for placing anywhere you need a temporary kennel area, such as the kitchen or family room. Like a crate, it is essential for safely confining your Border Collie when you cannot give him your undivided attention—when you are eating, working on the computer, or doing the laundry.

If you place the exercise pen in the kitchen area—or wherever your family tends to congregate—your puppy can get used to the many sights, sounds, and smells from the safety of his exercise pen.

Food Dishes

Your dog might consider these the most important on your list of supplies for him. After all, mealtimes are some of a dog's best times, and you will want to be sure your puppy or dog has bowls for both food and water.

Like other doggie essentials, there are plenty of bowls to choose from, and they are available at most pet outlet stores, feed stores, grocery stores, and online vendors. You can have a lot of fun with the selection, but there are a couple of things to keep in mind to make everyone's lives healthier and easier, though. The bowls you select should:

- be easy to clean
- not slip when they are placed on the floor
- be made of material that is not potentially harmful.

To meet these criteria, you should focus on stainless steel or heavy ceramic bowls—so long as the ceramic is finished with non-toxic glaze. The stainless steel is especially easy to clean, and most models come with rubber on the bottom to keep them from sliding.

As mentioned, you will need two bowls:

The Privileges of ILP

The Indefinite Listing Privilege (ILP) is a program offered by the AKC that allows owners of purebred dogs without pedigrees, which includes purebred rescue dogs, to be listed with the AKC and to participate in a variety of companion and performance events, including agility, herding tests and trials, junior showmanship, obedience trials, rally trials, and tracking tests. Dogs must have a veterinary certification of spaying or neutering to be considered. Owners complete an application and attach a clear front-and side-view photo of the dog in a standing position. A committee determines whether or not the dog is eligible for ILP registration.

You will want to protect your dog by putting an I.D. tag on his collar and microchipping him.

one for water, and one for food. You must have a bowl of clean, fresh water available for your Border Collie at all times. Rinse the bowl and refill several times a day, and thoroughly clean it as least once a day. Your dog's food bowl should be cleaned before and after his regular meals.

Identification

Identification, be it an I.D. tag, tattoo, or microchip, is essential. There are several options from which to choose, and each has their pros and cons.

Tags

Your Border Collie must have an I.D. tag that includes your name and telephone number. It is relatively inexpensive and well worth the investment because it's your Border Collie's ticket home should he become lost or separated. Tags are readily available at retail pet outlets, mail order catalogs, and online vendors. They come in a variety of shapes, sizes, colors, and materials, and easily attach to your dog's buckle collar with an S clip or good-quality split ring. You can even find nameplates that attach directly to your dog's collar, eliminating the unmistakable, not to mention frequently annoying, jingling noise produced by multiple tags dangling from a dog's collar.

Microchipping

Until recently, tattooing was the most widely used method of permanently identifying an animal. Twenty years ago tattooing was modern technology in terms of canine identification. Dogs were tattooed on their belly, however the numbers were often difficult to read—especially when done by the inexperienced. Modern technology has given dog owners peace of mind in the form of a microchip. It is a silicon chip, also called a transponder, about the size of a grain of rice that is painlessly inserted under your dog's skin. The microchip contains an unalterable identification number that is recorded in a central database along with your name, address, and telephone number. The microchip is scanned and the identification number is read via a hand-held electronic scanner. A universal scanner can now detect and read the numbers of all major brands of microchips. The majority of veterinary clinics and humane societies have universal scanners, and within seconds a microchipped dog can be identified. However, a microchip will not do your Border Collie any good if it is not registered. So don't forget the paperwork! Several state and national registries are available for registering and storing your contact information.

Leashes

Like collars, leashes are an essential piece of equipment for any dog owner. They come in a variety of choices, but when all is said and done, choosing a leash is usually a matter of personal preference. Nylon leashes are lightweight and relatively inexpensive, and it never hurts to have an extra one in the car, motor home, or around the house. They come in every color of the rainbow and can even be personalized with your name and telephone number. They work great for smaller dogs and young puppies, but are not always the best choice for medium or large dogs because they are hard on your hands and can slice your fingers to the bone, should your dog lunge or give a good pull.

Leather leashes are quite a bit more costly but often worth the investment when you own a Border Collie. Unlike nylon leashes, leather leashes are kinder and gentler on your hands, which is important because you'll be using it a lot, and the more you use it, the softer and more pliable it becomes. A good quality, well cared for leather leash will be around long after your Border Collie has settled into his golden years.

When purchasing a nylon or leather leash, be sure to buy one that is appropriate for the size of your dog. A lightweight nylon leash suitable for an adult Bichon Frise may work temporarily on a Border Collie puppy, but it will do you no good on an adult dog. Generally, a five-eighths or three-quarter inch wide leather or nylon leash will provide sufficient strength and control as your dog grows bigger and stronger.

Retractable leads are designed to extend and retract at the touch of a button. They allow you to give your Border Collie plenty of distance on walks without carrying a long line that can get tangled, dragged through the mud, or wrapped around bushes. A retractable lead that extends to 16 feet (480 cm) allows your Border Collie plenty of privacy

The Paper Trail

When you purchase a purebred Border Collie you are entitled to certain types of paperwork. At the very least, you should receive a bill of sale and a pedigree. Most reputable sources will provide you a bill of sale, three-generation pedigree, registration certificate, health certificate, and sales contract.

to do his business or explore an open field while you lag behind. A single-finger brake button allows you to stop your dog at any time. Retractable leads are also ideal for teaching and reinforcing the come command. If you go this route, be sure to invest in a good quality retractable lead, designed specifically for big, strong dogs, that should last a lifetime.

Toys

Border Collies, like all dogs, not only enjoy chewing, they need to chew, especially puppies, who will experience teething as their baby teeth erupt and fall out. Again, there is a vast and seemingly endless selection of dog toys available, and you and your Border Collie can have a lot of fun selecting favorites. Your healthiest and most long-lasting selections, however, will be toys made for your Border Collie's body type and chewing power. Hard nylon and rubber toys are made for real gnawing and gnashing. They exercise your dog's teeth and gums, promoting oral health while relieving the need to chew. You can learn more about the best types of these toys for your Border Collie on the Nylabone website.

Be careful with plush toys that contain squeakers or noise-makers. Border Collies can chew right through the material and may swallow the squeaker, which could become lodged in the throat.

There are many kinds of edible chews for dogs that provide nutritional enhancement or breath fresheners. Most are strong enough for your Border Collie to get a good chew out of before breaking into bits that can be eaten. These should not be substitutes for the more long-lasting chew toys, but they make an enjoyable break for

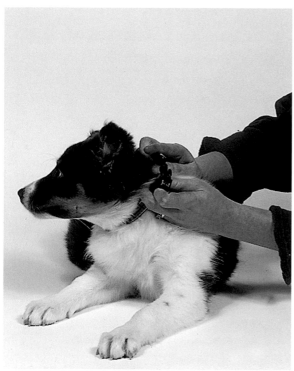

Buckle collars made of leather, nylon, cotton, or hemp are all fine for your Border Collie.

your dog. Always monitor your dog while he is chewing on bones or toys to prevent injurious incidents. Your veterinarian can help you choose the best chew toys and bones for your Border Collie's size and chewing habits.

TRAVELING WITH YOUR BORDER COLLIE

Border Collies love a good road trip, especially if the agenda includes spending time with their owners. Most Border Collies are adaptable and make wonderful travelers, but do not wait until you are on the road to discover yours is not! Ideally, it is best to accustom your Border Collie to traveling while he is young and more receptive to new adventures.

In the Car

For most Border Collies, riding in the family car is part of their everyday life, as natural as herding sheep. One of the best ways to accustom your new Border Collie to traveling is to put him in his crate and take him everywhere—weather providing, of course. Take him for a ride to the bank, post office, grocery store, to visit your friends and family, or to the vet's office for a cookie. Make it fun. Give him treats. Tell him he's wonderful.

For some dogs, however, riding in a car can produce a great deal of anxiety. They frequently will drool, shake, and even vomit. For dogs who have true motion sickness, which is normally associated with an inner ear problem, medications are available and can be used with the supervision of a veterinarian.

Carsickness, on the other hand, is usually associated with fear or an apprehension of the car noise and movement, a response to the dog's inability to control his circumstances, or a traumatic experience in a car or at the journey's end, such as an unpleasant experience at a vet's office or being left at an animal shelter. If your dog has problems riding in the car, you may want to begin reconditioning him by simply sitting in the car without the motor running, while you verbally praise him for being brave and reward him with tasty treats. When he shows signs of improving, sit in the car with the motor running while you verbally praise and reward him with yummy tidbits. Then begin with short, fun, and up-beat trips around the block, to the post office, bank, and so forth. Each time gradually increase the distance, always making the experience fun and positive. You can put a favorite blanket, toy or treat in his crate to keep him comfy and occupied.

Border Collies make excellent traveling companions, so it is well worth the training to help your dog overcome his fear of riding in a car. Doing so will allow you and your dog to enjoy years of fun and

Tag Tips

When choosing an engraved disc or nameplate, be sure to check it on a regular basis for readability. Stainless steel, brass, or gold-plated tags allow for deep engraving and maintain readability longer. Barrel-type identification tags allow you to write information on a piece of paper and insert it into the barrel that attaches to your dog's collar. When choosing this type of ID tag, be certain the barrel cannot come apart, causing your dog's information to become lost.

travel. It is worth noting that traveling with a Border Collie is not unlike traveling with a small child. You will need to make frequent pit stops to allow him to relieve himself, stretch his legs, and burn off a bit of pent-up energy.

If necessary, there are several over-the-counter products available at pet stores or in the pet section of health food stores. Typically, they contain flower essences, valerian extract or similar ingredients that have a calming effect on dogs. Dramamine is perhaps the most notable OTC medication. In severe cases, your veterinarian can prescribe a stronger, anti-anxiety medication. Always consult a veterinarian before giving your Border Collie tranquilizers, aspirins, or medication prescribed for humans.

By Air

Dogs traveling by air are protected by U.S. Department of Agriculture regulations. That in itself does not guarantee your pet will be safe flying the friendly skies. However, there are safety regulations and precautions to help minimize potential dangers, including the following:

- Dogs must be at least eight weeks old and be weaned prior to traveling.
- Dogs must travel in airline-approved crates that meet stringent USDA regulations for size, strength, sanitation, and ventilation. Your Border Collie may be refused a boarding pass if his kennel does not meet the government's requirements.
- A licensed veterinarian must examine your dog and issue a health certificate within ten days of traveling.
- Dogs flying outside the continental United States may be subjected to quarantine regulations.

Regulations vary from airline to airline, so it is important to always plan ahead. Not all airlines accept dogs, and many limit the number of dogs accepted on each flight. Call the airlines well in advance of your travel plans to schedule flights. Ideally, when booking a flight try to:

- Book nonstop flights during the middle of the week, avoiding holiday or weekend travel.
- Avoid as many layovers and plane changes as possible.
- During warm weather, choose flights early in the morning or late in the evening.
- In cooler months, choose midday flights.

Travel Tips

Never allow your Border Collie to travel with his head hanging out an open window or ride in the back of an open pick-up truck. Dust, debris, and bugs are an ever-present danger and can damage his eyes and nostrils. A sudden, unexpected stop could throw him from the car, causing serious injury or death. An unrestrained Border Collie may bolt from an open window or the back of a truck at the first sight of a field full of sheep!

An exercise pen is a handy way to confine your dogs when you can't give them your full attention.

Specific regulations for national and international air travel are available on the USDA webpage: http://www.aphis.usda.gov/ac

On Land

There is no limit to the number of places and the amount of fun you and your Border Collie can have when traveling together. Planning ahead is the key to a safe, fun-filled adventure.

Hotel or Motel

If your travels with your dog include staying at a hotel or motel, call ahead to be sure they take pets. Not all hotels and motels accept dogs—even well-behaved Border Collies. Some facilities allow dogs in the rooms but may require they be crated. Some larger hotels provide kennel facilities. Many require a refundable pet deposit or a nonrefundable pet fee.

Be a good ambassador for the Border Collie breed—as well as all dogs—by following hotel and motel rules, including never leaving an unattended dog in the room. An otherwise calm dog may become anxious in unfamiliar surroundings. He may chew furniture, shred pillows, urinate, defecate, or annoy other visitors with his barking. If you plan to have your Border Collie sleep on the bed, bring an extra sheet or blanket from home to cover and protect the motel's bedspread. Without exception, always clean up after your Border Collie and deposit any messes in designated trash bins.

Auto clubs usually list approved lodgings that accept dogs, and there are a number of guidebooks that list regional and national dog-friendly motels and hotels.

Campgrounds

Like hotels and motels, not all public or private parks and campgrounds allow dogs. Most recreational vehicle clubs provide directories that include a park's pet policy. However, these policies are subject to change, so it is highly advisable to call ahead. Be sure to follow park rules, and do not allow your Border Collie to intrude on other campers or their animals. It is never wise to leave your Border Collie unattended or tied out where he can be teased, stolen, or attacked by another dog or wild animals.

WHEN YOU CAN'T TAKE YOUR BORDER COLLIE WITH YOU

Unexpected business trips, family emergencies, and weather conditions that are too hot or too cold may exclude your canine friend from your travel plans. Unfortunately, not all hotels, motels, and resorts accept dogs—even well-behaved Border Collies. Whatever the reason, occasions may arise when you need to leave your Border Collie for a few days or a few weeks. Yes, it's heartbreaking, but there are several options that may give you peace of mind.

Boarding Facilities

Boarding facilities have come a long way in the last 10 or 15 years. Many are now designed with the discriminating pet owner in mind, and they provide a variety of services in addition to boarding, including training, daily exercise, and grooming. Some facilities provide video cameras that allow you to view your Border Collie via a laptop or PC.

Your Border Collie's physical safety and emotional well-being are paramount. Here are some tips for reducing yours and your Border Collie's stress by choosing the best facility:

- Visit and tour the entire facility. A clean and inviting reception area does not guarantee clean kennel runs. If the proprietors do not want you touring the facility—hightail it to the nearest exit.

Buckets of Water for Cooling Off

Border Collies like to cool off by jumping into a trough of water or a kiddy pool. Having one readily available for your Border Collie will ensure he has plenty of opportunity to cool off and prevent him from overheating.

- Check the cleanliness of the kennels, runs, and exercise areas. Are they free of debris and excrement? How often are the kennels cleaned? How are they cleaned and disinfected between boarders? Does the kennel or exercise area smell?
- Check the security of the facility. Is it completely fenced? Double fenced? Do the kennels and exercise yards have good latches? Are the fences sturdy and at least six feet high?
- Where will your Border Collie be boarded? Indoors? Outdoors? Or a combination of the two? Are the indoor facilities heated? Are the outdoor facilities protected from the weather?

There are now insured pet sitting organizations around the world that will watch your dog in your home for you while you're away.

- What will your Border Collie be sleeping on? Do you need to bring his bed or favorite blanket?
- If you have several Border Collies, can you kennel them together? Is there an additional cost to do so?
- How frequently will your Border Collie be walked or exercised? For how long? What type of exercise? Does someone interact or play with him? Or is he simply left unattended in an exercise yard with or without other dogs?
- Will your Border Collie be housed with other dogs? This can be extremely dangerous and stressful to your Border Collie, especially if the combination is not compatible. A young dog may be bullied or roughed up by an older dog who may be an aggressive, overexcited, or rambunctious kennelmate.
- Is there a veterinarian or 24-hour emergency clinic nearby?
- What are their admission and pick-up hours? What happens if your return is delayed?
- What vaccinations are required?

Once you have decided on a facility, remember to book early. Many facilities are booked months in advance, especially during the holidays. Always leave special pet-care instructions, your itinerary, and numbers to contact you or a trusted friend or relative in the event of an emergency.

Pet Sitters

If boarding your Border Collie is out of the question, you might want to consider a pet sitter. No doubt he'll still miss you, but there is a good chance he will be less stressed in the comfort of his own home surrounded by your scent and his prized possessions. He will be happier sticking to his normal routine, or as close to normal as possible, eating his regular diet, sleeping in his own bed, playing with his favorite toys, and lounging in his favorite spot. You may be lucky enough to have a responsible neighbor, trusted friend, or relative you can rely on to stop by several times a day; but if not, you might want to seek out the services of a professional pet sitter.

Pet sitters are people who either stay at your home while you are gone or stop in during the day to feed, exercise, and check on your dog. Ask your dog-owning friends, local veterinarians, trainers, or groomers for a referral.

Travel Checklist for Your Border Collie

When traveling, do not forget to pack a few necessities for your dog:

- Your Border Collie's current health certificate and rabies inoculation.
- Current photographs of your dog, to be used for identification should he become lost.
- An extra leash, collar, and set of ID tags.
- An adequate supply of food, water, and feeding dishes.
- A pooper-scooper, paper towels, or plastic bags for picking up after your Border Collie.
- Medications and prescriptions.
- Chew toys, bones, tug toys, balls, and the like.
- A favorite blanket or bed.
- An adequate supply of doggie towels for quick cleanups, in the event your Border Collie gets wet, dirty, or injured.

If you choose the pet sitting route:

- Have the pet sitter come to your home for an interview. Is she professional? Did she show up on time?
- How does she relate to your Border Collie?
- How much experience does she have? Will she be able to recognize if your dog is sick or having a problem?
- If she is not staying at your house, how often will she come by? Once a day? Three times a day?
- Will she play with your Border Collie? Talk to him? Kiss him? Love him?
- Is she licensed? Bonded? Insured?

Doggie Daycare

Doggie daycare is becoming increasingly popular. They are similar to daycare centers for human babies but with a twist. They are for dogs! If you want Border Collie to play, interact, romp, and tussle with other dogs while you are at work—doggie daycare may be your cup of tea.

Daycare centers vary in their appearance, amenities, and cost. Some resemble park-like atmospheres with trees, park benches, kiddy pools, and playground equipment. Some facilities provide spa-like amenities and lavish the dogs with attention, including hydro-baths, nail trims, and massages.

To find the right daycare facility for your Border Collie, consider the following:

• Always visit and tour the facility. Is it securely fenced? Clean?

• What type of services do they provide?

• What type of supervision do they have? How many dogs are assigned to each person?

A supply of sturdy chew toys will exercise your dog's jaws and mind.

• Are puppies and small dogs separated from large dogs?

• Are quiet, timid dogs separated from rambunctious, overzealous dogs?

• Do they have a place for your Border Collie to get away from the other dogs?

• What type of training or experience do the employees have?

• Where will your Border Collie spend his day? Indoors? Outdoors? In play groups?

• What vaccinations are required?

• Is there a veterinarian or emergency clinic nearby?

Once you have decided on a daycare facility, always leave a telephone number where you or a trusted friend or family member can be reached in the event of an emergency.

FEEDING
Your Border Collie

The old adage, "You are what you eat" applies to your Border Collie just as much as it applies to you. Feeding a complete and balanced canine diet is the first and most important step in providing your dog with the necessary nutrients to live a happy, healthy life. Equally important, do not believe the rumor that suggests what is good for you must also be good for your dog. Dogs and humans have different nutritional requirements, and a number of human foods can cause life-threatening medical problems for dogs.

Studies indicate that proper nutrition can help prevent disease, promote healthy skin and coat, and provide your Border Collie with optimum health and longevity. While a trip to the pet food aisle can seem more intimidating than learning computer science, feeding your four-legged friend a well-balanced diet is nothing to be afraid of. All it really requires is a basic understanding of canine nutrition, a keen observation of your Border Collie and whether or not his diet is agreeing with him, and finally, the ability to look beyond the slick multimillion-dollar ad campaigns.

THE BASICS

When it comes to nutrition, all dogs are not created equal. Some dogs have allergies to certain food sources, such as beef, chicken or fish, which can cause an array of troubles, including scratching and intestinal gas. Others are sensitive or intolerant to poor-quality ingredients and grain-based diets. One of the most important requirements in feeding your Border Collie is to look at his individual nutritional needs and then feed a diet that provides the correct combination of nutrients. What works for one Border Collie may not work for another because a dog's nutritional needs will change depending on his age, environment, housing conditions, exposure to heat or cold, overall health, and the emotional and physical demands placed upon him. Some Border Collies are in constant motion, and the more active

Your Border Collie's nutritional needs will change as he grows and becomes more – or less – active.

the dog, the more energy he burns. As a result, active dogs require a higher intake of nutrients to fuel their bodies. Think of it as premium gasoline in a well-tuned sports car. A working Border Collie, for instance, will require more calories than the family pet who runs and plays with the kids for a few hours each day. If your senior Border Collie's primary job is guarding the couch, he will not require as many calories as an agility competitor. A pregnant or lactating bitch's nutritional requirements will differ from that of a ten-year-old spayed Border Collie.

To help your Border Collie's complex system run efficiently, it is important to find the diet that provides the correct balance of nutrients for his individual requirements.

Your Border Collie's diet is likely to change several times over the course of his lifetime. However, the nuts and bolts of canine nutrition remain the same. There are six basic elements of nutrition: carbohydrates, fats, minerals, proteins, vitamins, and water.

Carbohydrates

Dogs are omnivorous animals, meaning they eat both animal and vegetable foods, and they get most of their energy from carbohydrates. Carbohydrates are the energy foods that fuel your Border Collie's body. Scientific research indicates that up to 50 percent of an adult dog's diet can come from carbohydrates. They are often referred to as *protein-sparing* nutrients because the action of carbohydrates (and fats) in providing energy allows protein to be used for its own unique roles.

Soluble carbohydrates consist mainly of starches and sugars and are easily digested. Insoluble carbohydrates, better known as fiber, resist enzymatic digestion in the small intestine. Fiber, while important to the overall process, is not an essential nutrient.

Carbohydrates are introduced in the diet primarily through vegetable matter, legumes, and cereal grains, such as rice, wheat, corn, barley, and oats. Unused carbohydrates are stored in the body as converted fat and as glycogen in the muscles and liver. In the absence of adequate carbohydrates, your Border Collie's system is able to utilize fat and protein as a form of energy. However, protein is less efficient because the body does not make a specialized storage form of protein as it does for fats and carbohydrates. When protein is used as an energy source—rather than to do its unique job of building muscle, regulating body functions, and so forth—the body must dismantle its valuable tissue proteins and use them for energy.

Fats

Fats and oils are the most concentrated sources of food energy in your Border Collie's diet. Fats account for approximately 2.25 times more metabolizable energy—the amount of energy in the food that is available to the dog—than carbohydrates or proteins. Fats play an important role in contributing to your dog's healthy skin and coat and aid in the absorption, transport, and storage of fat-soluble vitamins. Fats also increase the palatability of foods, but they contain more than twice the calories of proteins and carbohydrates. Just like your own diet, fats in your Border Collie's diet should be regulated. Dogs seldom develop cardiovascular problems that are associated with humans, but consuming too much fat can result in excess

Working dogs like Border Collies, especially, need food that supplies the nutrients they need to keep them going.

calorie intake, which is not good for your Border Collie's health or waistline.

Minerals

Not too many people get excited about minerals. You seldom hear diet gurus gushing about minerals like they do with fats, carbohydrates, and proteins. Minerals do not yield sources of energy, but they are important in the overall nutritional equation because they help regulate your Border Collie's complex system and are crucial components in energy metabolism.

Minerals are classified as macro minerals or micro minerals depending on their concentration in the body. Micro minerals, or trace elements, include iodine, iron, copper, cobalt, zinc, manganese, molybdenum, fluorine, and chromium, which dogs need in very small amounts. Macro minerals are needed in large quantities and include sodium, potassium, magnesium, calcium, and phosphorous.

While any dog should have free access to cool water during the day, a working Border Collie will need a great deal.

Essential nutrients must be obtained from your Border Collie's food because his body cannot make them in sufficient quantity to meet physiological needs. If dogs get too much or too little of a specific mineral in their diets, it can upset the delicate balance and cause serious health problems including tissue damage, convulsions, increased heart rate, and anemia. You should never attempt to supplement minerals in your Border Collie's diet without professional advice from a veterinarian.

Contaminated Water

It is worth noting that infectious agents and diseases, such as leptospirosis, Giardia, and E.coli can be transmitted through contaminated water. To greatly reduce the risk of disease, do not allow your Border Collie to drink from puddles, streams or ponds, as the water could be contaminated with parasites that could make him ill.

Protein

Proteins are compounds of carbon, hydrogen, oxygen, and nitrogen atoms arranged into a string of amino acids—much like the pearls on a necklace. Amino acids are the *building blocks* of life because they build vital proteins that develop strong muscles, ligaments, organs, bones, teeth, and coat. Protein also defends the body against disease and is critical when it comes to the repair

and maintenance of all the body's tissue, hormones, enzymes, electrolyte balances, and antibodies.

There are ten essential amino acids that your Border Collie's body cannot make on his own or make in sufficient quantities. These amino acids must be obtained through his diet. To make protein, a cell must have all of the needed amino acids available simultaneously because the body makes complete proteins only. If one amino acid is missing, the other amino acids cannot form a partial protein. If complete proteins are not formed, it reduces and limits the body's ability to grow and repair tissue.

Vitamins

A dog's body does not extract usable energy from vitamins, but they are essential as helpers in the metabolic processes. Vitamins are vital to your Border Collie's health and available in food sources, but they can be easily destroyed in the cooking and processing of commercial dog foods. Certain vitamins are dependent on one another with nearly every action in a dog's body requiring the assistance of vitamins. Vitamin deficiencies or excesses can lead to serious health problems, such as anorexia, artery and vein degeneration, dehydration, muscle weakness, and impairment of motor control and balance.

Vitamins fall into two categories: water-soluble (B-complex and vitamin C) and fat-soluble (A, D, E, and K.) Unlike humans, dogs can make vitamin C from glucose so they do not need to acquire it in their diet. All other water-soluble vitamins must be replenished on a regular basis through diet. Fat-soluble vitamins are absorbed and stored in the body, which makes over-supplementation potentially dangerous. Seek your veterinarian's advice and read as much as you can before supplementing your dog's food.

Water

One seldom thinks of water as an essential nutrient. However, it is the single most important nutrient needed to sustain your four-legged friend's health. Water regulates your Border Collie's body temperature, plays an important part in supporting metabolic reaction, and acts as the transportation system, so to speak, that allows blood to carry vital nutritional materials to the cells, and remove waste products from your dog's system.

The amount of water a dog needs to consume daily will vary from dog to dog depending on growth, stress, environment, activity, and age. A dog's need for water increases as he expends more energy during work, exercise, play, or training because dissipation of excess heat from a dog's body is accomplished largely by the evaporation of water through panting. If the weather is warm, the amount of water he requires will increase. If your Border Collie eats primarily dry dog food, he will need access to fresh water to help aid in the digestion.

Rather than trying to estimate your Border Collie's daily water requirement, it is best to provide him with access to an abundant supply of fresh, cool drinking water at all times. When dogs have free access to water they will normally drink

Premium Vs. Cost-Conscious Foods

There is no substitute for good nutrition. For maximum health and longevity, a dog must be properly fed and cared for throughout his life. Choosing a premium food over a bargain or generic brand food makes good nutritional and economic sense. Across the board, premium foods tend to be nutritionally complete, meaning they have all the required nutrients in balanced proportion so your Border Collie is getting adequate amounts of all required nutrients. Premium foods are also developed to provide optimal nutrition for dogs during different stages of life, such as puppy, maintenance, active, and senior diets. The initial investment for a premium food is a bit higher on a per weight basis, but because they tend to be higher in digestibility and nutrient availability, less food is required per serving.

enough to maintain the proper balance of body fluids. If you have less than desirable city water or are concerned about fluoride, chlorine, or lead in your water supply, consider a filtration system or try boiling water or purchasing bottled water for your Border Collie.

WHAT TO FEED YOUR BORDER COLLIE

When it comes to feeding your Border Collie, there are many different options available. From convenient commercial food to healthy home-cooked meals, the most important thing to remember is to find a diet that works for you and your dog. Make sure you speak to your vet before making any drastic changes to your Border Collie's diet.

Most people choose to feed their Border Collies a commercially prepared food for the convenience.

Bones & Raw Food Diet (BARF)

It is not difficult to find proponents and opponents on both sides of the controversial issue of whether a BARF diet is best for dogs. Ask a dozen people and each one is sure to have a different opinion. Essentially, some owners believe that raw bones and foods are more suitable for their dog than highly processed foods because they believe drying, freezing, heating, or canning robs food of its nutritional components. The concept appears to stem from the desire to return to a more *natural* style of living and to feed a *pure* diet, similar to what wild dogs might have eaten long ago.

There are two challenges with this type of diet: First, it is difficult finding a good source of healthy raw meat and bones, and then achieving the correct balance of nutrients—water, vitamins, minerals, protein, carbohydrates, fats—in the right amounts, and doing so on a routine basis. Second, dogs who eat raw bones, particularly chicken and turkey bones, are highly susceptible to choking or damaging their stomachs. Both of these situations can be life threatening. In addition, dogs, like humans, are susceptible to internal parasites, bacteria, and food-borne illnesses caused by raw meat, poultry, eggs, and unprocessed milk.

High-quality commercially prepared dog foods are available for different growth stages.

Feeding a raw food and bones diet works for some owners. However, feeding this type of diet should be undertaken only after a great deal of research and understanding, and it is highly recommended you work closely with a veterinarian or certified canine nutritionist.

Advantages
- You control the ingredients.
- Proponents believe dogs live longer, have healthy lives, and better immune systems.

Disadvantages
- Time consuming to prepare.
- Difficult to find fresh, high-quality raw meats.
- More expensive—especially if using organic foods.
- Difficult to achieve complete and balanced levels of nutrients on a regular basis.

- Concern of bacterial infections, parasites, and food-borne illnesses for both dogs and humans when handling and eating raw foods (i.e., E.coli and Salmonella).
- Choking hazards when eating raw bones.

Commercial Diets

Commercial diets are undoubtedly the most convenient foods to buy, store, and use. They are readily available and when compared to homemade diets they are definitely less time consuming. Most major dog-food manufacturers, and a number of veterinary hospitals, have invested enormous sums of money in researching and studying the nutritional requirements of dogs in different stages of life. As a result, they are quite knowledgeable about the requirements of puppies, adult dogs, athletic dogs, pregnant bitches, and senior dogs, and what constitutes good canine nutrition.

It is also important to keep in mind that the commercial dog food industry is a multibillion-dollar-a-year business. Advertising experts spend a significant amount of time researching, developing, and marketing products in a manner to convince you to buy a particular brand. This is not necessarily bad, but it is important to keep in mind if you are choosing a food because of the creative advertisements and fancy packaging rather than nutritional requirements of your dog.

Canned Foods

Canned foods are mostly water—approximately 75 percent. They contain more meat than a dry diet and little to no grain.

Advantages
- High palatability.
- Easier to digest.
- Contains a higher meat protein level.

- Canning process kills harmful bacteria.
- Long shelf life.

Disadvantages
- More expensive than dry foods.
- Provides no abrasion from chewing, which allows faster plaque and tartar build-up on teeth.
- Requires refrigeration after opening.
- High heat processing can destroy some nutrients.
- Due to high water content, moist foods have fewer nutrients than other foods. More food must be eaten to satisfy energy and nutrient needs.

Your dog may be begging for a homemade diet, but consider the expenses of time, money, and overall nutritive value when thinking about switching.

Dehydrated Foods

Dehydrated foods, which contain fresh meats, grains, and vegetables, are dehydrated at low temperatures to preserve all the natural nutrients.

Advantages
- Once dehydrated, foods can last indefinitely.
- Easy to store.

Disadvantages
- Can be costly.
- When rehydrated, the food becomes a moist mixture.
- Does not provide abrasion or scraping while chewing.
- Does not satisfy a puppy's need to chew.

Dry Food

Dry foods, commonly called "kibble," contain between six to ten percent moisture (water) and a high percentage of carbohydrates in the form of grains.

Advantages
- Economical, readily available, and convenient to buy, store, and use.
- Good shelf life. Does not require refrigeration.
- May improve dental hygiene through chewing and grinding, which aids in the removal of dental plaque. Although this is highly

debatable among the experts. (Does not eliminate the need for regular dental care.)
- Provides some exercise for a dog's mouth, and helps satisfy a puppy's need to chew.
- High-quality brands have high caloric density and good digestibility, which means lower amounts per serving need to be consumed.
- Stool is usually smaller and more compact.

Disadvantages
- Less palatable to some dogs than canned or semi-moist foods.
- High heats used in the processing stage can destroy valuable nutrients.

Semi-moist Foods

Semi-moist foods are often shaped into patties and come in a prepackaged size convenient for feeding. They are generally marketed in sealed and re-sealable pouches. They are 25 to 35 percent water. Ingredients can include fresh or frozen animal tissues, cereal grains, fats, and simple sugars. It is worth noting that semi-moist foods can contain propylene glycol, an odorless, tasteless, slightly syrupy liquid used to make antifreeze and de-icing products. Propylene glycol is generally recognized as safe by the FDA for use in dog food and other animal feeds. It is used to absorb extra water and maintain moisture, and as a solvent for food coloring and flavor.

Advantages
- High sugar content may increase palatability.
- Less offensive smell than canned foods.
- Good shelf life. Does not require refrigeration.

Disadvantages
- High sugar levels in dog food cause spikes in blood sugar levels and contribute to obesity.
- High sugar levels may aggravate an existing or borderline diabetic condition.
- Contains high levels of salt.
- Contains propylene glycol.
- Sticky, sugary foods can contribute to dental disease.

Prescription Diets

Prescription diets are special-formula diets prepared by dog food manufacturers and normally available only through a licensed veterinarian. They are designed to meet the special medical needs of dogs, such as low protein and mineral diets for kidney disease, low protein, magnesium, calcium, phosphorous for bladder stones, lamb and rice based diets for food-induced allergies, and low calorie foods for weight-reduction diets.

- If left out for long periods of time, such as in a dog bowl, it will dry out, reducing palatability.

Homemade Diets

Let's face it, unless you are schooled in canine nutrition and you have an abundance of time and energy on your hands, feeding a homemade diet is easier said than done. Preparing your Border Collie's food from scratch is a romantic and selfless notion. After all, who does not want the best for their dog? What owner does not want to feed foods free of preservatives, additives, and who knows what else?

Truth be told, homemade diets are a time consuming, labor-intensive, expensive, and complicated process. It is tricky, albeit not impossible, to prepare a canine diet on a daily basis that is complete and balanced and contains the proper ratio of nutrients. Do you know the calcium / phosphorous ratio in the diet you are preparing? It is important stuff. The nutritional value of raw ingredients will fluctuate depending on their sources, and supplementing with vitamins and minerals is usually necessary. However, too much or too little or the wrong combinations of supplements can be harmful

to your dog. If you are so inclined, you could mix all the food ingredients, supplements, treats, snacks, and so forth, into a blender and have the sample professionally analyzed.

The bottom line is when you choose to feed a homemade diet you assume full responsibility for the nutritional status of your Border Collie. If this is what you decide to do, it is prudent to consult with a veterinarian or certified veterinary nutritionist before proceeding

Advantages
- You control the ingredients.
- You can customize by providing a mixture of fresh meat, chicken, fish, vegetables, and commercial kibble.
- You can provide a combination of cooked and raw ingredients.

When your dog is on a regular feeding schedule, he will anticipate – and look forward to – mealtime.

Disadvantages
- Time consuming to prepare.

- More expensive—especially if using organic ingredients.
- Difficult to achieve complete and balanced levels of nutrients on a regular basis.
- Concern of bacterial infections, parasites, and food-borne illnesses for both dogs and humans handling and eating raw foods (i.e., *E.coli* and Salmonella).

SCHEDULED FEEDING VS. FREE-FEEDING

When it comes to feeding your Border Collie, there are two options: scheduled feeding, which is highly recommended, and free feeding, which is more convenient for you, but not nearly as beneficial for your dog.

Scheduled Feeding

You will need to feed your puppy at regular times. Whatever food is left after 15 minutes, you should pick up and, if necessary, refrigerate any perishable food or throw away leftovers to prevent spoilage. This regimen will help your puppy establish a regular routine of eating and eliminating, which will help speed up the housetraining process. Designated feeding times can also help with the bonding process. Your puppy learns food comes from you— the pack leader. It also helps to avoid obesity in your puppy. Juvenile obesity increases the number of fat cells in a puppy and predisposes him to obesity for the rest of his life.

Free Feeding

Free-feeding, which is

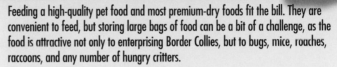

Storing Dog Food

Feeding a high-quality pet food and most premium-dry foods fit the bill. They are convenient to feed, but storing large bags of food can be a bit of a challenge, as the food is attractive not only to enterprising Border Collies, but to bugs, mice, roaches, raccoons, and any number of hungry critters.

Oxygen, heat, humidity, and light are also major sources of damage to dog food. All-natural foods and foods with natural preservatives generally have a shorter shelf life because preservatives, such as vitamin E, tend to break down quicker than artificial preservatives. Dry foods usually have a shelf life of one year, and canned foods are normally good for two years, but be sure to check the "best if used by" date on the bag or can.

Proper storage of foods can help maximize the food's shelf life and eliminate exposure to most environmental factors, including mold, heat, humidity, and light, as well as insect infestation, rodents, and other animals. Ideally, to preserve freshness, you should store opened bags of food in a container with a tight fitting lid that minimizes the food's exposure to air or potential infestation. Specialized pet food storage bins ranging from portable to stackable to plastic to nylon are available at most pet stores and online vendors. Some Border Collies are quite talented when it comes to prying the lids off containers, so be sure the container you choose is truly dog proof. Plastic or rubber-type bins work well, but be certain to purchase bins intended specifically for storing food. If possible, keep dry food in its original bag, placing the opened bag inside the container. If not stored in a container, roll the top of the bag down and secure it with several clips to keep out insects and other pests. Store both dry and canned foods at room temperature, and never above 90 degrees. Fahrenheit (32 degrees Celsius). Remember, heat is a major culprit in food spoilage and nutritional degradation. Storing foods below 50 degrees Fahrenheit (10 degrees Celsius) may change the consistency and palatability of the food, but should not alter the nutritional value. Moisture encourages the growth of mold, so avoid storing dry foods in basements and bathrooms. Once opened, canned foods should be covered with a tight-fitting lid, refrigerated, and used within three days.

putting the food out, leaving it all day, and allowing your puppy to eat at his leisure, is not recommended because it does not establish a set schedule for feeding and eliminating. While a few dogs are able to regulate their food intake, most dogs will eat and eat and eat as long as food is available. After a good vomit, they gleefully start all over again. If food is available continuously, some dogs will develop the annoying and potential dangerous habit of food-bowl guarding. Finally, if you have multiple dogs, it is best to confine all of them separately in crates or kennels while they eat. Otherwise, you will not know for certain if your puppy is eating or the other dogs are eating for him. More important, even the best of friends are likely to squabble over food.

AGE-APPROPRIATE FEEDING

Your Border Collie's caloric requirements will change as he matures, growing bigger and stronger, and again when he begins to enter his senior years. Feeding the appropriate foods through his life stages will help to keep him healthy and happy.

If you have more than one, each of your Border Collies should have his own food dish and be supervised at meal times.

Feeding Your Border Collie Puppy

A Border Collie puppy has gigantic nutritional demands. Besides the fact that a puppy spends a significant part of his day playing, which requires a lot of calories, his body is growing rapidly. His system is building strong muscles, bones, and vital organs, and establishing a resistance to disease. As a result, for the first 12 months of his life he needs a specially formulated growth food that is designed exclusively for his greater energy and nutritional needs.

A growing puppy needs about twice as many calories per kilogram of body weight as an adult Border Collie. Since puppies have small stomachs, they also need to be fed smaller amounts of food three or four times a day until they are about six months old. From six months to one year of age and thereafter, you should feed your Border Collie two times a day—once in the morning and again in the evening.

Growth rates and appetites of puppies are primarily dictated by genetics and will vary from puppy to puppy, so feeding the correct amount can be a bit tricky. The feeding guidelines on puppy foods are just that—guidelines. They are not etched in stone, and many dog food manufacturers tend to be overly generous with their proportions. Your veterinarian can help you determine the proper amount to feed.

For the first few days after bringing your precious pooch home, you should continue feeding the same type and brand of puppy food he has been eating, provided he has been eating a well-balanced, good-quality puppy food. Depending on where and from whom you purchase your Border Collie, this may or may not be the case.

Feeding Your Adult Border Collie

Different breeds of dogs reach maturity at different ages. As a general rule, smaller breeds tend to reach adulthood sooner than large breed dogs. It is highly likely your Border Collie will reach adulthood around 12 months of age. That said, the age of maturity varies from Border Collie to Border Collie, with some reaching maturity sooner or later than others.

Adult foods, often called maintenance diets, are specially designed foods that satisfy the energy and nutritional needs of adult dogs who have reached maturity. These diets are designed to provide the proper quantities of nutrients to support a mature Border Collie's lifestyle. Border Collies who are very active, under physical or emotional stress, or lactating have different nutrient requirements than the average canine couch potato. Your veterinarian can help you determine when and what type of adult food to choose. Most experts recommend feeding an adult dog twice a day—once in the morning and again in the early evening. As with puppies, pick up any food left after 15 minutes and refrigerate or toss it.

Feeding the Senior Border Collie

Different dogs age at different rates, and determining if and when you should begin feeding a senior food will depend on your individual dog. It is impossible to arbitrarily set an old-age age. You cannot randomly say that Border Collies are old at eight or nine years of age. Dogs age differently, depending on their genetics and overall lifestyle.

A good rule of thumb used by many veterinarians is to divide the average lifespan of a Border Collie into thirds. When your Border Collie is in the last one-third of his life, he is usually considered an

Switching Foods

If you intend to switch foods, it is best to do so slowly to prevent intestinal upset. Veterinarians recommend switching foods over the course of seven to ten days to prevent upset stomachs, vomiting, loose stool, or constipation. To do this, make a mixture of 75 percent old food and 25 percent new food. Feed this mixture for three or four days. Then make a mixture of 50 percent old food and 50 percent new food. Feed this mixture for three or four days. Then make a mixture of 25 percent old food and 75 percent new food. Feed this mixture for three or four days. Then you can start feeding 100 percent new food.

Be Smart Before You Buy

To help you purchase quality products and reduce your chances of getting taken for a ride at the cash register, follow these tips:

- Buy from a trustworthy company that has a reputation for producing a quality product.

- Investigate the company before buying their product. How long have they been in business?

- Does the company have veterinarians or animal professionals on staff? Who at the company is answering your questions? Are they educated in animal physiology?

- Nutraceuticals are not hip replacement in a bottle. If it sounds too good to be true, it probably is.

- Cheaper is not always better. Don't buy a product simply because it costs half as much as other products.

- Don't believe everything you read on the Internet.

older dog. For instance, using that simplified mathematical equation and considering the average Border Collie lifespan is between 12 and 14 years (give or take a year), the average Border Collie would be considered an older dog around 8 or 9 years of age. Again, there are exceptions to every rule and some Border Collies remain physically and cognitively young at 10, 12, or 13 years of age.

Older dogs usually require a diet that is still complete and well balanced, yet lower in calories, protein, and fat. In some instances, you may be able to feed your Border Collie his regular adult food but in smaller quantities. Or you may need to switch to a diet designed specifically for senior dogs.

Because older dogs do not normally get as much exercise as their younger counterparts, losing weight can be difficult for them. Maintaining a sensible weight throughout your Border Collie's entire life is one of the most important and humane things you can do to help your dog retain good health and increase the quality and length of his life. Knowing this ahead of time, you can plan ahead and take precautions that do not allow your Border Collie to become overweight at any stage of his life.

On the other side of the spectrum, older dogs will occasionally go off of their food, meaning they lose interest in it, and may choose to eat only once a day. If your Border Collie is losing weight or his eating habits have changed, it is important that a veterinarian examine him to rule out any possible disease problems. Because dogs age at different rates, it is best to work closely with a veterinarian as your Border Collie begins to enter his senior years. Your veterinarian can help you determine the specific nutritional and supplemental needs of your Border Collie in this stage of his life.

NUTRITIONAL SUPPLEMENTS

In most cases, if you are feeding a quality diet that is complete and well balanced, supplementing in not recommended or required. Some owners just like adding stuff to their dog's feed, and they occasionally supplement with yogurt, brewer's yeast, fish oils, vegetables, broths, and even canine multi-vitamins. You may not

If your Border Collie is not overweight, don't allow him to become so.

consider this supplementing, but a supplement is anything that is given in addition to a dog's feed.

Your Border Collie's system is complex, and to run efficiently it must receive the proper amounts of nutrients in a balanced ratio. By supplementing, you may inadvertently upset that intricate balance. Fat-soluble vitamins, for example, are stored in a dog's body, so it's easy to upset their nutritional balances. That said, a dollop of yogurt, a splash of chicken broth, or a squirt of fish oil is not likely to upset that intricate balance. However, you should always consult your veterinarian before adding multi-vitamins or mineral supplements.

OBESITY

Not too many working Border Collies have a problem with excess weight. After all, they spend the majority of their time in constant motion—working livestock, running, jumping, and being silly. That's not to say Border Collies don't get fat. They do, and one is more likely to see weight issues with Border Collies in non-working or companion homes.

Like humans, dogs who carry around extra pounds are subject to serious health issues including diabetes, increased blood pressure, congestive heart failure, and digestive disorders. Fat works as an insulator, which is great if you're a hibernating bear, but on a

Border Collie too much fat will wreak havoc with his internal and external parts. For starters, extra fat restricts the expansion of your Border Collie's lungs, making breathing difficult. Overweight Border Collies are less capable of regulating their body temperatures and therefore more susceptible to heatstroke than their lean counterparts. Overweight Border Collies have less stamina and endurance because their heart, muscles, and respiratory system are working overtime. Keep reading—there's more! Overweight Border Collies have increased surgical risks, decreased immune functions, and are more susceptible to injuries including damage to joints, bones, and ligaments. Simply put, overweight and obese Border Collies have a diminished quality of life, and they tend to die at a younger age than their physically fit counterparts.

Is My Border Collie Overweight?

A good, well-balanced diet is a sure way to keep your Border Collie fit, lean, and happy, and can increase his lifespan by nearly two years! Generally speaking, most adult male Border Collies weight around 45 or 50 pounds, and females between 35 and 45 pounds. That said, Border Collies differ in size, bone structure, and muscularity, so it is impossible to arbitrarily set a correct weight for all Border Collies. You can't, for instance, say all females should weight 45 pounds, and males 50 pounds. Some Border Collies have

Your dog will be happy to be with you on picnics in the park; just watch that too many leftovers don't go his way.

thick coats that can be deceiving. So you will need to put your hands on your dog and feel his neck, ribs, and hips. To be sure your Border Collie is not packing extra pounds, follow these simple guidelines for assessing your Border Collie's weight:

- Pinch the skin on his neck—just ahead of his shoulders—between your thumb and finger. Ideally, your fingers should be no more than ¼ inch apart.
- Run your fingers up and down his ribcage. You should be able to feel the bumps of his rib cage without pressing in.
- Run your hand over his croup (his rump). You should be able to feel the bumps of his two pelvic bones with little effort and without pressing down.

Some owners think if they can feel their Border Collie's ribs, he's too thin. Not so! You want your Border Collie to be fit and lean. Not too skinny, but not too fat. Ideally, when looking at your dog from the side, his abdominal tuck—the underline of his body where his belly appears to draw up toward his hind end—should be evident. When standing over your dog and viewing him from above, his waist—the section behind his ribs—should be well proportioned. An overweight Border Collie will have a layer of fat covering his ribs, and you will have difficulty feeling them. His abdominal tuck may still be present, but his waist from above, will be more difficult, if not impossible, to distinguish. If your Border Collie is very overweight or obese, his appearance alone should be a good indicator. You won't be able to feel his ribs because of the fat covering them. He'll probably have fat deposits on his back and hip region, spine, chest, shoulders, neck and legs. His tummy will hang down, and his belly may look distended.

Your veterinarian can help you determine the ideal weight for your Border Collie, and develop a long-term plan to condition his body and provide him with a longer, healthier life.

The Battle of the Bulge

How can you help your Border Collie fight the battle of the bulge? If your Border Collie is currently overweight or obese, the first step should be a trip to the veterinarian. Some medical conditions, such as hypothyroidism and Cushing's disease, can contribute to weight gain, but those cases represent a very small portion of overweight dogs, perhaps less than five percent, according to experts. Some medications, such as prednisone and phenobarbital, can influence a dog's metabolism and appetite. A veterinarian can examine your Border Collie to assess his overall health and medical condition, and can advise you on sensible and healthy ways to reduce your Border Collie's weight.

It is easier to keep the weight off than it is to take it off. If your Border Collie is not overweight—do not allow him to become overweight. It's that simple. In the long run it is the kindest thing you can do for him. Border Collies who are overweight as young dogs are at a greater risk to become overweight adult dogs.

Feeding the Right Food

To keep your Border Collie's figure fit and trim, you need to choose the food that best suits his activity level and life stage. Overweight and underweight dogs, as well as puppies, athletic, and geriatric dogs have different nutritional and caloric requirements. Puppies require specially formulated diets. An older, less active Border Collie will generally need fewer calories than a young, energetic Border Collie, and an overweight Border Collie may require a special-reduced calorie diet. When in doubt, always seek veterinary assistance in choosing the food that best suits your Border Collie.

Table Scraps

If you find yourself sneaking your precious pooch a tidbit of

His request may appear to be irresistible, but giving in will only lead to begging.

steak or a French fry or two from the supper table, you will need to grow a thick skin and ignore his woeful and pleading stares. Feeding table scraps is one of the worst ways to sabotage your dog's weight maintenance program. A tasty tidbit of steak here, a nibble of chicken there, a potato skin, a French fry or two—what's the harm, right? It is better for table scraps to go to waste than to your Border Collie's waist. If you absolutely cannot resist feeding table scraps, put them in the refrigerator and feed them at a later time as a training treat. Feeding from the table also encourages begging, which is a difficult habit to break.

Treats

James Spratt was an electrician who lived in America for many years, but he achieved fame in the canine world when he began making dog biscuits in London during the mid-1800s. Today, some 145 years later, the number of commercial dog treats available is mindboggling! When choosing treats, it is important to read labels carefully and choose treats that are low in fat, sugar, and salt. Small pieces of fruit or fresh veggies are good alternatives to store bought treats. Or try baking your four-legged friend some yummy, low fat, homemade treats. Treats should be a reward for a job well done, such as coming when called. Treats should never be a substitute for well-deserved hugs and kisses.

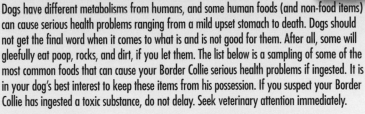

Foods to Die For

Dogs have different metabolisms from humans, and some human foods (and non-food items) can cause serious health problems ranging from a mild upset stomach to death. Dogs should not get the final word when it comes to what is and is not good for them. After all, some will gleefully eat poop, rocks, and dirt, if you let them. The list below is a sampling of some of the most common foods that can cause your Border Collie serious health problems if ingested. It is in your dog's best interest to keep these items from his possession. If you suspect your Border Collie has ingested a toxic substance, do not delay. Seek veterinary attention immediately.

- Alcoholic beverages can cause intoxication, coma, and, in some instances, death.

- Bones from fish, poultry, or other meat sources can cause obstruction or laceration of the digestive system.

- Cat food, while not fatal, is high in protein and fat and particularly appetizing for enterprising Border Collies. Too much can cause intestinal upset and unnecessary weight gain.

- Chocolate. Oh, so yummy for people, but deadly for dogs. It can increase a dog's heart rate and breathing, resulting in serious illness and death.

- Grapes and raisins contain an unknown toxin, which can damage your Border Collie's kidneys.

- Macadamia nuts contain an unknown toxin, which can affect your Border Collie's digestive and nervous system, and muscles. A double dose of trouble is chocolate covered Macadamia nuts!

- Mushrooms can contain toxins that vary depending on the species. They affect multiple systems resulting in shock and death. They grow in the wild—and your backyard. Closely supervise your dog to prevent ingestion.

- Onions and garlic contain sulfoxides and disulfides, which can be toxic to dogs. They can damage red blood cells, causing anemia.

- Tobacco contains nicotine and can cause an increased heartbeat, collapse, coma, and death.

Chapter

5

GROOMING
Your Border Collie

G rooming your Border Collie on a regular basis not only keeps his skin and coat in tip-top condition, but also allows you to check his entire body for lumps, bumps, cuts, rashes, dry skin, fleas, ticks, stickers, and the like. You can check his feet for cuts, torn pads or broken nails, and examine his mouth for tartar, damaged teeth or discolored gums. Regular grooming will improve your Border Collie's appearance, and since most dogs love to be groomed, this makes the necessary chore a great way to spend quality time with your dog while simultaneously building a strong and mutually trusting human/ canine relationship.

For the household or working companion, as opposed to the show dog, grooming is a relatively easy process as long as it is done regularly, and the dog views it as a positive and enjoyable experience.

If you have a Border Collie puppy, it is a good idea to start good grooming practices right away. If your puppy came from a reputable breeder, he is probably used to being handled and gently stroked. He's probably had at least one bath and may already be accustomed to and tolerate being brushed and examined. A puppy who is exposed to positive and delightful grooming experiences will grow into an adult dog who takes pleasure in the regular routine. Few things are as frustrating as trying to wrestle down a 50-pound Border Collie who hates to be groomed.

GETTING YOUR BORDER COLLIE USED TO GROOMING

If grooming is new to your Border Collie, don't despair. Like anything else, it is best to start slow and progress at a rate that is suitable for the age and mental maturity of your dog.

If you have a grooming table, begin by teaching your Border Collie to stand on the table. For a puppy, any sturdy surface such as a bench or crate top covered with a non-skid, non-slip surface is sufficient.

Border Collies are pretty agile, and jumping on and off a grooming table can be a fun game for them, but they also run the risk of injuring themselves—especially if they are jumping onto hard concrete or slick surfaces.

An adult Border Collie may be too heavy for some people to lift, but don't discard the grooming table! Teach your dog "feet up"—which is to put his front feet on the grooming table, then you can boost his back legs up and onto the table. (This works great for boosting dogs into SUV's, vans, and larger cars.) Most dogs learn "feet up" when owners pat the table and say the command "feet up." When the dog puts his feet up—praise and reward. If he doesn't get the hang of "feet up," simply lift his front feet onto the table then hoist his rear legs up. Getting off is a bit trickier. Most owners employ a lifting and jumping combination. Put one of your arms between your dog's front legs, and your other arm wrapped under his chest/stomach area. As the dog jumps, your arm positioning helps guide him and cushion a hard landing.

Some companies manufacture ramps specifically for loading dogs in and out of cars, onto grooming tables, etc. If you are handy with a hammer and nails, you could make your own or build a couple of building block-type boxes that he can walk up onto the table and then off again.

Sitting or kneeling on the floor with your Border Collie works in a pinch, too. In addition, it is prudent to have all of the grooming tools out and within easy reach *before* you start grooming. You never want to turn your back or leave your Border Collie on a grooming table unattended. A young Border Collie can easily be injured should he fall or jump.

Puppies have limited attention spans, so do not expect your Border Collie to stand still for extended periods of time. In the beginning, you want progress—not perfection. Your goal is for him to stand still for a few seconds while you praise him. Harsh handling during these learning stages will only build resentment toward the necessary chore. Progress to the point where your puppy will accept having his body stroked with your hand, then gently, slowly, and calmly brush him all over. In the beginning, your Border Collie may be frightened, nervous, or unsure. Patience and kind handling will help to build his confidence and teach him to accept and enjoy the grooming process.

A common mistake owners make is to turn grooming into a game, or to allow the dog to make it a game. Grooming should definitely be a positive and pleasant experience, but a dog who decides grooming is a game is likely to become overstimulated and nip or bite at the hand that grooms him. It is best to put a stop to that behavior right away, as it can become an established behavior that is difficult to break.

BATHING

How often your Border Collie requires bathing will depend on where you live, how much time he spends outside, and how dirty he gets. If he is a working dog, or simply your constant companion on walks, jogs, hikes, and trips to the barn or pasture, he may require bathing on a regular basis, say, every four to six weeks or so. If he spends a great deal of time indoors, he may require bathing once every three or four months. There is no cut-and-dried formula for how often your Border Collie needs bathing. You will need to be the judge.

Most Border Collies enjoy the water and are quite amenable to baths. In hot climates, you may be able to bathe your dog outdoors with a garden hose, provided the water is not too cold. Otherwise, a rubber mat on the bottom of a bathtub or shower stall will provide secure footing and prevent him from slipping. Don't forget the slippery floors, either. A rubber mat or plenty of dry towels on the bathroom floor will prevent your dog from slipping and injuring himself as he jumps out of the tub. You might consider investing in a grooming apron—or a raincoat! Border Collies love to shake when they are wet. So have plenty of towels on hand for wiping down walls, mirrors, and fixtures. You might also want to buy an inexpensive screen that fits over the drain opening. This will help to keep your dog's excess hair from clogging the drains.

Unless your dog has a specific skin condition, such as dry, flaky, itchy skin, choose a mild shampoo designed specifically for dogs. Some shampoos contain harsh detergents that can dry the skin and damage the coat by stripping it of natural oils. Look for

Your Border Collie will revel in a good shake after his bath.

While your dog may think so, charging through puddles doesn't count as a bath – though it may lead to getting a real one in the tub!

shampoos that are natural, non-toxic, and biodegradable. There are many shampoos and conditioning products from all-purpose to medicating to herbal to color enhancing, so do not be shy about asking for help when choosing shampoos and conditioners.

How to Bathe Your Border Collie

A lot of Border Collies will gladly jump in to the tub when asked to do so. Some are less agreeable, and you will need to physically place them in the tub. If you are using your bathroom tub, it's usually easier to slide your arms under his tummy (like a forklift sliding its hooks under a pallet), lift him up, step into the tub while holding him, and then gently place him in the tub, all the while being careful not to slip and fall or, heaven forbid, drop him. If you are lucky enough to have a grooming area or a large sink in the laundry room, use the forklift technique and simply lift him into the tub. For larger Border Collies, you may need to purchase or construct a ramp that your dog can walk up and into the tub.

Saturate your Border Collie's topcoat, undercoat, and skin with lukewarm water. This can take some time if your dog has a thick coat. A cotton ball placed in each ear will keep the water out. Apply a dab or two of shampoo and scrub away! Work the shampoo into the coat with your fingers or a rubber massage tool designed specifically for dogs. Scrub from head to toe, being careful to avoid getting soap in his eyes. Always use tearless shampoo to gently wash around the head and eye area. This will prevent any irritation should soap accidentally get in his eyes. If this happens, don't panic. Simply rinse his eyes thoroughly with a cool, low-pressure stream of water. Most likely he won't open his eyes, so do the best you can to rinse them.

Don't forget to scrub his belly, the inside of his hind legs, and under his arms. Rinse his entire body thoroughly with warm water—then rinse again and again until the water runs clear. The rinsing is the most important part.

A Border Collie's coat can hold a lot of suds, and residual shampoo can irritate the skin, as well as leave a dull film on the coat. If necessary, shampoo and rinse again to be sure your Border

Collie is squeaky clean! If you are using a coat conditioner or skin remoisturizer, be sure to follow the directions carefully.

If possible, let your Border Collie shake off any extra water, then towel dry him thoroughly.

Throughout the entire bath and until he is completely dry again, protect him from any drafts. If you live where the temperatures are warm and your Border Collie is likely to air dry quickly, blow-drying is usually not necessary. If you decide to use a blow dryer (human or special canine blow dryer), hold the dryer at least six inches away from the coat, keep the dryer in motion, and use a low or cool heat setting to avoid damaging the coat or burning your dog's skin.

It is worth noting that wet Border Collies love to roll in whatever is handy, be it grass, dirt, mud, or gravel. You might consider keeping him sequestered in the house until he is dry. Otherwise, before you can say "squeaky clean"—your precious pooch is likely to have undone all of your hard work!

BRUSHING

The Border Collie is double-coated—meaning he has a longer outer coat (or top coat) and a soft, dense undercoat that develops as the dog reaches adulthood. For most Border Collies, a pin brush—a wire-pin brush with or without rubber tipped ends—for long hair, a slicker brush with bent wire teeth for removing mats, dead and shedding hair, and a steel comb with teeth divided between fine and coarse for removing debris, are sufficient for day-to-day grooming and whisking away pieces of debris, dust, dirt, and dead hair.

A Border Collie's double coat means he sheds, and the amount of shedding—which is a natural process where strands of hair die, fall out (shed), and are replaced by new hairs—varies according to the dog, the season, and climatic conditions. Most Border Collies shed heavily in the spring or early summer when they tend to blow coat. You "strip" a dog's coat when the undercoat has died. A stripping comb will help pull out the dead hairs from the undercoat, which allows the new coat to grow in more quickly. Several stripping session may be necessary to remove all of the undercoat. If possible, do this outdoors as it makes quite a mess.

This champion show dog has been groomed to perfection.

Grooming Tidbit

After bathing your Border Collie, be sure his collar and neck areas—especially the throat area—are thoroughly dry before putting his collar back on. A wet nylon or leather collar pressed against wet fur is an ideal site for bacteria growth. Equally important, if your Border Collie swims in the family pool, ocean, ponds, rivers, streams, and the like, be sure to remove his collar until his neck and collar area (and his buckle collar) are completely dry. This will help to prevent bacteria and the unmistakable doggie odor that frequently accumulates in these areas. If your Border Collie regularly swims in a chlorinated pool or in rivers, streams, and ponds—you may want to rinse him afterward to prevent skin irritations.

Regular brushings are essential for whisking away these dead hairs, promoting and distributing natural oils, and bringing out the shine and natural luster in a dog's coat. Regular brushings also prevent the undercoat from matting. If a matted coat gets wet, the moisture is trapped near the skin, causing hot spots—circular lesions that are inflamed, raw, moist, and very painful.

When properly cared for on a regular basis, a Border Collie's coat is relatively easy to maintain. Like anything else, however, if neglected, it can take the better part of a year to restore it to a good and healthy condition.

Brushing a dry coat can cause hair breakage and damage. Therefore, throughout the brushing process, regularly mist or spray the hair with a coat dressing, a coat conditioner diluted with water, or plain water. This will help to protect the hair and control static as you brush.

How to Brush Your Border Collie

Some breeders and groomers recommend starting at the dog's head—brushing the top of the head and around the ears, down the neck, chest, and front legs. Then brush in one long stroke from the head toward the tail, and then down the sides and finishing with the rear legs. Others prefer starting at the feet and working upward. Many groomers discourage backward brushing—brushing against the direction of hair growth—because it can damage the coat, and some dogs find the process uncomfortable and annoying. Either way, be sure to brush down to the skin, brushing both the top coat and undercoat. Brushing only the top coat can result in painful mats and tangles that are difficult, if not impossible, to comb out.

Some Border Collies, especially males, can have quite a lot of feathering on their legs—the hair that runs from the elbow to the pastern (or wrist) area. Everything from dirt to mud to snowballs to freshly mowed lawn clippings accumulate in leg featherings. It is important to keep this area brushed and cleaned to prevent painful mats and coat damage. Consider trimming the feathering short for convenience sake. It can save you a lot of time and energy, especially during the wet and snowy weather.

Pay attention to the soft fuzzy hair behind the ears, too. It mats easily, so it needs to be kept cleaned and brushed regularly. Thinning the fuzzing hair will help to prevent matting while keeping your dog's coat tidy. Place the thinning shears under the top coat and make a few snips—thinning the undercoat rather than the top coat—then brush to remove the trimmed hair.

Remember, your Border Collie's skin is sensitive, despite his brawn! Brush gently; don't tug or pull, as this can hurt. Part the hair with one hand and work from the skin out with the brush. Be careful not to brush the skin itself with a slicker brush, as this can create nicks, scratches, and even welts—often referred to as "slicker burn."

Regardless of which method you choose, once-a-week brushings are usually sufficient. However, a five-minute once-a-day once over with a pin or slicker brush is ideal and will help keep your Border Collie's coat glossy and gorgeous, and keep shedding to a minimum.

The double-coated Border Collie needs a pin brush, a slicker brush, and a comb to get through all his hair.

You can finish the coat and add shine by applying a small amount of specially designed coat dressing or coat oil. This will protect the coat from the elements and help to prevent burrs and debris from sticking to the coat.

As you brush, pay particular attention to the condition of his coat. A Border Collie's coat is a mirror reflection of his health. Check to see:

- Is your Border Collie's coat healthy and shiny? Or is it dull, brittle, and lackluster?
- Is his skin dry and flaky?
- Does it have a bad smell or that unmistakable doggie odor?
- Do you see bare spots where hair is missing?

Any of these conditions could be a sign of inadequate grooming, internal illness, parasite infestation, or an inadequate diet. When in doubt, a veterinarian can diagnosis the problem and recommended suitable treatments.

DENTAL CARE

Just as you take good care of your teeth, it is essential that you take good care of your Border Collie's teeth. The importance of high-quality dental hygiene cannot be overstated. If left unattended, your Border Collie can develop periodontal disease, a progressive disease that can, in advanced cases, lead to decayed gums, infection, and liver, kidney, and heart damage. It is one of the most frequently

Doggie Bad Breath

Also known as halitosis, bad breath is generally indicative of something more serious, such as periodontal disease, diabetes, kidney disease or gastrointestinal problems. Unless you have seen your precious pooch eat something particularly offensive like spoiled garbage, squirrel guts, cat stools or another dog's stools, or even his own stools—yes, some dogs find this appetizing—it is best to have your dog examined by a veterinarian. If left untreated, some causes of bad breath, such as periodontal disease, abscess, kidney, gastric or metabolic disease can cause severe and even fatal complications.

diagnosed health problems in dogs with an estimated 80 percent of dogs over the age of three having some stage of periodontal disease. And like humans, dogs do experience painful toothaches, although some dogs—especially Border Collies who tend to be very stoic—may not physically exhibit signs of pain, or the signs may be subtle and therefore overlooked by some owners.

Dental Problems

Dental problems in dogs begin the same way they do in humans—with plaque. Plaque is a mixture of salivary glycoproteins—in layman's terms, a colorless, translucent adhesive fluid or slime—and the major culprit in periodontal disease.

Gingivitis and Periodontal Disease

Plaque begins with the accumulation of food particles and bacteria along the gumline. Germs present in plaque attack the gums, bone, and ligaments that support the teeth, and daily, routine home care helps to remove plaque. However, when left untreated, minerals and saliva combine with the plaque and harden into a substance called tartar, or calculus. As tartar accumulates, it starts irritating your dog's gums and causes an inflammation condition called *gingivitis*, which is easily identified by the yellowish-brown crust on the teeth and the reddening of gums next to the teeth.

In the early stages, periodontal disease, which results from the buildup of plaque and tartar around and under the gumline, is generally reversible provided your Border Collie receives veterinary attention along with sufficient and regular brushings at home. Otherwise, the process continues to erode the tissues and bones that support the teeth, which can lead to pain and tooth loss. As bad as that sounds, it can get worse.

If the tartar is not removed, the cycle continues to repeat itself, encouraging even more bacterial growth. The tartar builds up under the gums, causing them to separate from the teeth and causing even larger pockets where more debris can collect. At this stage, your Border Collie's teeth no doubt have quite an accumulation of highly-visible, crusty yellowish-brown tartar. Brushing your Border Collie's teeth on a regular basis will remove plaque, but not tartar. If your Border Collie already has a tartar build up, he will need to see a veterinarian to have it removed and his teeth inspected, cleaned, and polished.

In most advanced stages, damage from periodontal disease is considered irreversible because bacterial infection has been busy destroying your Border Collie's gums, teeth, and bones. Treatment, which can include difficult and extensive surgeries, will not reverse the damage, but it is essential to prevent progression and to guard against bacteria entering the bloodstream, causing secondary infections that can damage your dog's heart, liver, and kidneys. Treatment will also help eliminate much of the pain your Border Collie is experiencing. Imagine living with a toothache for several years!

Fractured Teeth

Fractured teeth can cause your Border Collie a great deal of pain, especially if the broken tooth exposes the pulp—the soft inner portion of the tooth containing the blood vessels and tissues. If left untreated, bacteria can lodge in the damaged tissue causing countless problems ranging from inflammation to abscesses.

Border Collies can break their teeth in any number of ways and on any number of objects, such as chewing on rocks, chain link enclosures or bones and chew toys that are too hard. Automobile accidents and dog fights can also lead to broken teeth. Working dogs may fracture their teeth while herding.

All teeth are subject to fracture, and frequently a broken tooth is visible—especially if it is a canine or incisor. Other times, the fracture may be below the gumline and not visible. Owners may notice symptoms, such as bleeding or pain when the tooth is touched. Some dogs will have difficulty eating and may avoid chewing on one side, or they may not drink very cold water. In some cases, dog will show signs of discomfort or lethargy.
Treatment depends on which parts of the tooth are broken. Serious breaks may require extraction or reconstructive surgery not unlike people receive, such as root canals and crowns.

How to Brush Your Border Collie's Teeth

As with other aspects of grooming, it is much easier to begin introducing oral hygiene to a puppy, but it is never too late to begin. You will need to start slowly and progress at a pace suitable for your Border Collie.

What You'll Need

You will need a pet toothbrush, gauze for wrapping around a

Oral problems contribute to overall poor health – something this happy, healthy dog doesn't have to worry about (yet).

finger, or a finger toothbrush, which, as the name suggests, simply slides over your finger, and some toothpaste designed specifically for dogs. If you go with a pet toothbrush, be sure to get one specially designed for a Border Collie or the mouth of a medium-size dog. A small toothbrush designed for, say, a Boston Terrier, will do little for your Border Collie. A word of caution: Do not use human toothpaste. It is not designed for dogs and can upset your dog's stomach. Most canine toothpastes are formulated with poultry or malt flavored enhancers for easier acceptance.

Dental Care

Many experts compare the structure of a dog's teeth to that of an iceberg. What you see above the surface is the tip of the tooth—or the "tip of the iceberg," so to speak. The structure of the tooth that lies below the surface is much larger, and it is easy to ignore what you cannot see. Unfortunately, by the time you notice an accumulation of tartar on the surface of your dog's teeth, you can be certain damage below the surface of the gums is well under way.

In addition to home care, a good dental hygiene program includes an annual veterinary examination. A veterinarian will check for potential problems, such as plaque and tartar build-up, gingivitis, periodontal disease, fractured or abscessed teeth. If necessary, a veterinarian may recommend professional dental cleaning, also known as prophylaxis or prophy. While anesthetized, a dog's mouth is flushed with a solution to kill bacteria, the teeth are cleaned to remove any tartar, polished, inspected, and flushed again with an antibacterial solution, and fluoride is applied. In most cases, X-rays will also be taken.

The best way to prevent periodontal disease is to keep your Border Collie's teeth clean, and brushing is one of the most effective ways of removing plaque. The process is relatively simple and requires nothing more than a small number of fairly inexpensive supplies and a few minutes of your time.

Most dogs, be they young or old, will no doubt take issue with a toothbrush being jammed in their mouth, so start by using your finger to gently massage his gums. Put a small dab of doggie toothpaste on your index finger and let your dog lick it. Praise him for being brave! Apply another dab on your finger, gently lift up his outer lips, and massage his gums.

Ideally, it is best to massage in a circular motion, but in the beginning you may need to be satisfied with simply getting your finger in your dog's mouth. Try to massage both top and bottom, and the front gums, too. Watch out for those sharp baby teeth, and remember to keep a positive attitude, and praise and reassure your Border Collie throughout the process. It is also helpful if you try to avoid wrestling with your dog or restraining him too tightly. This will only hamper the process and make him resistant to the necessary routine.

Depending on your dog, it may take a few days or a few weeks for him to accept you fiddling about in his mouth. Hopefully, he will eventually come to look forward to the routine. That is the long-term goal. It is possible he may never come to enjoy it, but it is important that he learn to accept it as part of his daily life.

Once your dog is comfortable with this process, try using a toothbrush, finger toothbrush, or a gauze pad wrapped around your finger. Let your dog lick some toothpaste off the toothbrush or gauze pad and, again, praise him for being brave! This will help accustom him to the texture of the brush or gauze while building his confidence.

You are now ready to begin brushing. As before, lift the outer lips and expose the teeth. Most owners find it easiest to start with the canine teeth—the large ones in the front of the mouth. They are the easiest to reach and you should be able to brush them with little interference or objection from your dog. Once your dog is accustomed to you brushing a few teeth, progress to a few more, then a few more until you have brushed all 42 teeth (or 28 teeth, if you have a puppy).

How Often to Brush

Ideally, you should strive to brush your Border Collie's teeth on a daily basis, just like you do with your own teeth. Like anything else, the hardest part is getting started. However, once you accustom your Border Collie to having his teeth brushed, you can incorporate it into your daily schedule. For instance, you might try incorporating it into your nightly routine, such as before you go to bed. You can make a production of it so your dog views it as a fun game you do together. Ask him in a happy, excited voice, "What are we going to do now?" Or, "Is it time to brush your teeth?" When you are done brushing, praise him for being brave! If brushing every day seems an impossible task, try to brush your dog's teeth every other day or at least several times a week because bacteria generally re-establish within about 20 minutes and tartar will harden within one or two weeks. If your Border Collie refuses to cooperate despite your best efforts—take him to your veterinarian for bi-annual or annual cleanings, which are done under general anesthesia. Your veterinarian can recommend the best timeline for regular cleanings.

EAR CARE

A Border Collie's ear canal is warm, dark, and moist, and that makes it an ideal site for bacterial or yeast infections, tumors, and parasites, such as ear mites. Unlike a human's ear canal, which is a basically a horizontal line from the side of the head inward to the eardrum, a dog's ear canal is L-shaped. The internal ear canal descends vertically before making roughly a 45-degree bend and then a horizontal stretch to the eardrum—also known as the *tympanic*

Why Anesthesia Is Necessary

For a complete and thorough oral examination and dental cleaning, your dog will need to be anesthetized. Regardless of how well your dog behaves—dogs do not tolerate thorough examinations, X-rays, probing, cleaning, flushing, and polishing of their teeth. While some proponents promote professional cleanings without the use of anesthesia, experts discourage this practice. Anesthesia is necessary in order to remove all the plaque and tartar from the crowns, below the gumline, between the teeth, and in the cases of periodontal disease, from between the roots of the teeth. Fractured teeth and wounds from bone fragments and wood splinters are sometimes impossible to see unless a dog is anesthetized. Equally important, professional strength fluoride, which is not safe to swallow, needs to be left on a dog's teeth for five minutes—a nearly impossible task with an awake animal.

A non-greasy, non-irritating ear-cleaning product designed specifically for dogs

Cotton or gauze pad

membrane. Debris loves to collect in the 45-degree bend of the ear canal.

The key to preventing ear problems is to keep them clean, and to know the difference between a clean-smelling ear and a problem ear. A healthy ear should have a clean, healthy doggie smell—resembling the smell of beeswax, somewhat. A honey-colored wax in the ear is normal, but a crusty, dark substance may indicate problems, such as ear mites. An infected ear has an unmistakable foul odor. Ear infections are serious and should never be ignored or taken lightly. If your Border Collie's ears have a discharge, smell bad, the canals look abnormal, red or inflamed, or your dog is showing signs of discomfort, such as depression or irritability, scratching or rubbing his ears or head, shaking his head or tilting it to one side—these can be signs of a problem. You should seek veterinary attention right away. An ear infection left untreated can cause permanent damage to a dog's hearing.

To help prevent problems, you should get in the habit of examining your Border Collie's ears regularly for wax, ear mites, and other irritations. If your Border Collie works, walks or plays in pastures, fields, or areas with heavy underbrush—check them frequently for stickers, burrs, and other foreign matters.

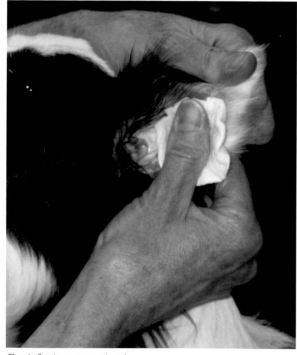

Ear infections are serious! Prevent them as best you can by regularly cleaning your Border Collie's ears.

How to Clean Your Border Collie's Ears

To remove dirt and debris, use an ear-cleaning product specifically designed for dogs. Place a few drops of cleaner into the dog's ear canal and then gently massage the base of the ear for about 20 seconds. This helps to soften and loosen the debris. At this point, it is okay to let your dog have a good head shake to eject the cleaning solution and debris from the ear canal. Next, apply some ear-cleaning solution onto a clean cotton or gauze pad. Gently wipe the inside ear leather (ear flap), and the part of the ear canal that you can see.

Remember the old adage, "Never stick anything smaller than

your elbow in your ear"? The same concept applies to dogs. Never stick cotton swabs or pointed objects into the ear canal because this tends to pack the debris rather than remove it. More importantly, you risk injuring your dog's eardrum should you probe too deeply.

If you suspect problems, seek veterinary attention right away and leave the probing to the experts.

EYE CARE

A Border Collie's eyes should be clear and bright, and can easily be cleaned by saturating a gauze pad with warm water, and then starting at the inside corner of the eye, gently wipe out toward the outside corner of the eye. If you notice excessive tearing, redness, swelling, discoloration, or discharge, these may be signs of an infection. If you suspect something is wrong, do not hesitate to call your veterinarian.

The sooner you get your puppy started on a grooming routine the easier it'll be to groom him as he grows. Make early sessions short and rewarding.

NAIL CARE

Nail trimming is a necessary part of dog ownership. Few Border Collies, especially those who spend the majority of their time indoors or on grass when outdoors, will wear down their nails naturally. If your dog's nails make the unmistakable *click, click, click* as he walks on hardwood, tile or vinyl floors—his nails are too long. Ideally, a dog's nails should not touch the ground. This allows a dog to stand squarely and compactly on the pads of his feet. Nails that are too long interfere with a dog's gait, making walking awkward or painful. Long nails can be broken, torn off or snagged, and can scratch furniture, hardwood floors, and skin. Torn or broken nails can cause a Border Collie a great deal of pain and discomfort, and they may become infected, which can require veterinary attention in order to remove the nail completely.

As with other aspects of grooming, it is best to introduce your Border Collie to the practice of nail care at a young age, as some dogs can be a bit fussy about nail trimming. With any luck, the breeder will have started nipping small pieces of nail as part of the socialization process, as well as to build the puppy's confidence and teach him to accept having his feet handled.

Puppies should have a minimal amount of discharge from their eyes, and it can be quickly wiped away with a tissue or your fingers.

If you choose to clip the nails yourself, it is highly advisable to invest in a good quality nail clipper designed specifically for dogs. In the beginning, depending on the puppy's level of cooperation, you may want to simply touch the nail clipper to the puppy's nail and then offer plenty of praise. Then progress to clipping tiny bits of nail during each session.

In the beginning, you may need someone to help hold your dog, but once you get used to it, trimming your Border Collie's nails is no more difficult than trimming your own. When in doubt, ask a veterinarian, groomer, or breeder to show you how to do it properly. Or have a professional trim them regularly, which can mean once a week or once a month—or somewhere in between—depending on the dog.

How to Cut Your Border Collie's Nails

Owners are often reluctant to trim their dogs' nails for fear of hurting the dog or making him bleed. Dogs have a blood vessel that travels approximately three-quarters of the way through the nail, called the "quick." Clipping a dog's nails too short can cut the quick and cause bleeding. However, learning how to do it properly, using the correct equipment, and having a dog who accepts having his feet handled, will go a long way in reducing the odds of inadvertently nipping the quick.

Your Border Collie may have white or black nails or a combination. Black nails can make it difficult to differentiate between the quick and the hook—the dead section of nail that extends beyond the quick. The quick travels approximately three-quarters of the way through the nail. As the nail grows, so too does the quick. For that reason, it is better to get in the habit of trimming tiny bits of nail on a regular basis rather than waiting for the nails to get too long and then expect to cut them back easily.

If you examine the underside of the nail before clipping, you will see that the section closest to the paw is solid, while the tip, or hook,

of the nail looks hollow like a shell. You may be able to see or feel the slightest groove on the underside hook portion of the nail. Trim only the portion between the solid nail and the thinner hollow part—just tipping it where it curves slightly downward. If accidentally nicked, the quick can bleed profusely and can be difficult to stop. There are a number of blood-clotting products available through retail stores, such as powdered alum, styptic powder, or styptic pencil. Having one of these products in your doggie first-aid kit is always a good idea.

If you accidentally cut the quick, your Border Collie will no doubt be a bit tentative about continuing with the process. However, it is important that you resist babying or coddling him. It is difficult not to bundle him in your arms and kiss and fuss over him, but this will only feed into his fear and nervousness. Do not scold or manhandle him either. It is best to play with him for a few seconds to take his mind off the incident. Proceeding with caution, clip one more nail, then stop the procedure and lavish him with praise and kisses, then brush a bit more, then clip another nail, then more kisses, more brushing, more clipping, more kisses, and so forth until the nails are completed. If your Border Collie has dewclaws, be sure not to overlook them in the trimming process. Dewclaws are the fifth digit on the inside of the front legs, usually an inch or so above the feet. If left unattended, they can curl around and grow into the soft tissue, not unlike an ingrown toenail on a human. Some breeders have the dewclaws removed, so your Border Collie may or may not have them.

Nail Care Supplies

Nail trimmer designed for dogs

Stypic powder or pen in case of bleeding

6

TRAINING AND BEHAVIOR

of Your Border Collie

Owning and training a Border Collie can be simultaneously exhilarating and exhausting. Some days, it can seem remarkably like the joys and frustrations of raising toddlers and teenagers! The good news is that training your Border Collie is a relatively simple process. Most of the problems you will encounter are entirely predictable, and armed with a good game plan and a bit of knowledge many problems are entirely preventable. At the very least, you can prevent them from escalating into major stumbling blocks.

BEHAVIOR TYPES

Understanding how dogs learn will greatly increase your chance of success and will help the training process move along much quicker. Canine genetics and animal behavior are complicated and exhaustive topics that go well beyond the scope of this book. The good news is you do not need a Ph.D. in genetics or animal behavior to figure out what makes your Border Collie tick. Without delving too deeply into the complexities of canine genetics, it is safe to say that dogs do what they do for two reasons: 1) inherited behaviors, and 2) acquired behaviors.

Inherited Behaviors

Inherited behaviors—also known as

genetic predispositions—are the traits that Mother Nature genetically preprogrammed. These traits are pretty much guaranteed to show up at some time in your dog's life whether you want them to or not. For instance, Border Collies were selectively bred as herding dogs, and the instinct to herd is in their genes. This inherent tendency to herd is part and parcel of your puppy's complete package. As a result, most Border Collies are high-energy. They also can be pushy and dominant.

By recognizing and understanding specific predispositions, you can learn to work within the confines of the breed—what the dog has and what he is built to do. You can learn to develop a particular style of handling in order to get the best from your particular dog, and you can design a training program that best suits your puppy's individual and inherited characteristics.

Acquired Behaviors

Acquired characteristics are behaviors your puppy has acquired from the day he was born. These behaviors are learned—be they

Your Border Collie's temperament will be the result of inherited and acquired tendencies. It will also be greatly affected by the socialization he receives.

good or bad, desired or undesired. Stealing food off the counter, refusing to come when called, peeing from one end of the house to the other, bolting out the front door, and committing heinous crimes against your personal property are all acquired behaviors. An eight-week-old Border Collie, for example, who learns to have fun chasing young children and nipping their pant legs will see no harm in doing this as a 50-pound (22.5 kilogram) adult dog. An adorable puppy who is mollycoddled every time he whines or barks will grow into an adult Border Collie who barks and whines whenever he wants attention. These are acquired behaviors—behaviors that a dog has acquired through learned experiences.

It is worth noting that acquired behaviors can also be positive behaviors. If, for instance, you call your six-month-old Border Collie and he comes tearing over to you with his head and ears up, his tail wagging and a happy attitude that screams, "Here I am!"—that too is an acquired behavior. The dog has learned to happily and eagerly come when he is called. Dogs who do not beg for food, steal food, bolt out doors, or run off have learned to respect their owners.

SOCIALIZATION

It is equally important to realize how important socialization will be to having a well-behaved pet. There are certain periods in a puppy's life that are critical in his social development. What happens within these individual stages has an enormous and significant impact on his future behavior as an adult. Research has shown that puppies are capable of learning at an early age, and they form lasting impressions during these critical periods. These impressions are remembered throughout a dog's life, be they good or bad.

A puppy who is exposed to positive experiences during the socialization period, such as handling, grooming, different sights and sounds, and so forth, stands a better chance of developing the socialization skills and coping mechanisms necessary to grow into a mentally sound and confident adult dog. Older puppies

Socialization begins at birth and builds from there. These youngsters are experiencing new toys and working with a photographer to have their picture taken. That's a lot!

who have not been adequately or properly socialized during these periods tend to be more cautious. They generally grow up shy, fearful, and frequently nervous. As adult dogs, they find it difficult if not impossible to cope with new experiences. They rarely, if ever, reach their full potential or live their lives to the fullest. This is a disastrous situation for Border Collies.

Socialization is the single most important process in a Border Collie's life. Breeders and owners owe it to their puppies to take advantage of these critical periods to maximize their future, foster their zany personalities, and instill desired behaviors. How much time and energy you invest during this critical period will directly impact the future character of your puppy.

Early Socialization

Socialization begins at birth, and good breeders have their work cut out as they labor daily to maximize and cement the future of their puppies. The *socialization* period, when a puppy is between 4 and 16 weeks of age, is pivotal in his development. During the first few weeks of this stage, the main emphasis of socialization begins to shift from your puppy's canine mother and his littermates toward human beings and the world beyond the whelping box. It is the prime time when your Border Collie learns to adjust to and interact with the presence of people in his life.

By the time your Border Collie puppy is ready to begin his new life at your home, usually between seven and eight weeks of age, the process of socialization will have already begun. The breeder will have seen your puppy through the *neonatal* and *transitional* periods, and halfway through the critical socialization period. During this time, responsible and knowledgeable breeders will ensure their litters are handled daily in order to accustom them to human contact and imprint trust, which is essential when it comes to raising a sound Border Collie. They may have a radio or television playing to accustom them to different voices and sounds. They will make sure the puppies receive individual attention and are exposed to a variety of sights and smells in a safe and stress-free environment. Many breeders will have accustomed their young puppies to crates, thereby facilitating the crate-training process.

This is why you need to make careful choices about where you acquire your Border Collie. How your puppy is managed during the neonatal, transitional, and socialization periods has a tremendous impact on how he reacts to various situations and people as an adult dog.

Your Role in Socializing Your Border Collie

Your job begins the day your puppy arrives at your home. There is much to accomplish and a very small window of opportunity, so it is important to maximize your time and use it wisely. There are important socialization skills your Border Collie must learn between 8 and 16 weeks of age. Once this window of opportunity has passed, it can never be recaptured. The lessons learned during this stage will help your Border Collie develop the socialization skills and coping mechanisms necessary to grow into a mentally sound and confident adult dog. If you dawdle or squander your opportunities during this critical time, your puppy will suffer in the long run. You run the risk of having your Border Collie develop bad habits and associations that are difficult, if not impossible, to correct later in life.

As the owner of a new Border Collie puppy, you are assuming the role of parent and pack leader. You are assuming an enormous responsibility that includes protecting him from bad or traumatic experiences while simultaneously instilling desired behaviors, fostering his zany personality, and providing him with every opportunity to grow into a well adjusted, mentally confident adult dog.

When exposing your impressionable pup to new people, places and things, be mindful of how he's reacting so he isn't unnecessarily frightened.

The importance of maximizing your opportunities during this critical period cannot be stressed enough. Puppies mature faster than humans. On the average, humans take about 18 years to reach maturity, while puppies take about one to one-and-a-half years, depending on the dog. Your eight-week-old Border Collie will be eight weeks old for exactly seven days. The same goes for being 9, 10, 11, 12 weeks old, and so forth. While one week may seem insignificant in the lifespan of a child, it represents a significant portion of your Border Collie's puppyhood. Once those seven days in each age span have passed, they can never be recaptured.

Therefore, if possible, it is advantageous to avoid scheduling vacations or extended trips out of town while your puppy is between 8 and 16 weeks of age—unless, of course, you plan to take him with you. Boarding him in a kennel or leaving him in the care of friends or relatives during this time puts your puppy at a serious disadvantage later on in life. You will have missed a prime opportunity to foster his zany personality, shape his future character, and instill all of the behaviors you want your puppy to possess as an adult dog.

How to Socialize Your Border Collie

Before taking your puppy outdoors and around other animals, you should consult your veterinarian about any necessary puppy vaccinations to ensure your Border Collie is protected from diseases. Then, in a fun, safe, and stress-free environment, you will want to begin exposing your Border Collie to a wide variety of people including children, teenagers, women carrying bags, men in floppy hats, other animals in the household, and so forth. You should expose your puppy to the clapping of hands, the jingling of keys, the clatter of dog bowls. He should explore a variety of surfaces including grass, cement, gravel, tile, carpet, linoleum, sand, and dirt. Many dogs—especially herding dogs—are attracted to moving objects, which incite their chase instinct. Your Border Collie should be exposed to these objects, including strollers, wheelchairs, shopping carts, vacuums, bicycles, and kids on roller skates and skateboards. A puppy who is not exposed to moving objects may be fearful of them and may try to attack them as he gets older.

He should be exposed to stairways, wheelchair ramps, paper bags blowing in the wind, wind chimes, and horns honking. Let your puppy play in and around empty boxes, tunnels, or buckets. Allow him to investigate trees, rocks, bushes, branches, leaves, and fallen fruit. He should explore bugs, and other animal odors, pastures, wooded areas, city sidewalks, and sandy beaches.

Enlarge your puppy's world and challenge his curiosity by taking him for rides in the car and walks in the park. Allow him to explore the many sights, sounds, and smells of a local dog show. Take him to the veterinarian's office or the local groomer for a cookie and a kiss. If you are interested in canine competition, expose him in a controlled atmosphere to the scents and sounds that he will encounter later in competition, such as agility or obedience equipment.

As the guardian of your puppy's safety and well-being, you will want to protect him from potentially harmful or fearful situations, yet not coddle or reward fearful behavior. You will want to observe your puppy's reactions to different situations. Watch his ears and tail and body posture. Is he fearful? Apprehensive? Courageous? Dominant? Submissive? By understanding and reading your Border Collie's body language, you will be able to evaluate and adjust the situation accordingly. For instance, if your Border Collie was raised in a childless environment, a room full of noisy, rambunctious children may be overwhelming or downright scary. By coddling or otherwise rewarding a puppy that shows fear, you are reinforcing his fear. Try modifying or restricting the exposure to one quiet, well-behaved child in the beginning until your puppy's confidence can handle more. When your puppy is brave, praise and reinforce him for being brave and inquisitive. "Good puppy!" or "Look at you. Aren't you brave!"

If you do nothing else for your puppy, you owe it to him to make the time to properly and adequately socialize him during this critical life stage. This may seem time consuming, but it is a necessary investment when you choose to own a Border Collie. His future well being depends on how much you do—or fail to do—during this critical period.

CRATE TRAINING

A crate is a fantastic training tool when used properly by responsible dog owners. Many owners look upon a crate as cruel

or inhumane. Instead, it should be viewed from a dog's perspective. Before dogs became domesticated pets, they tended to seek safe, enclosed areas for security and protection. A crate mimics that safe, enclosed environment. Puppies, especially very young puppies, tire quickly and need a lot of sleep during the day. A crate placed in a quiet corner of the kitchen or family room will replicate a dog's natural instinct to seek a safe and secure environment. When properly introduced, a crate becomes a safe-zone for your Border Collie—a quiet place all his own to sleep, eat, and retreat from the poking, prodding fingers of noisy, rambunctious toddlers.

Using the Crate

A crate, like any other training tool, has the potential to be abused. A crate is not intended for 24-hour confinement. Your Border Collie should live with you and not in his crate. A crate should never be used as a form of punishment. It should provide your Border Collie with a safe, secure environment, a place he enjoys.

Most puppies quickly learn to love their crates when it is associated with good things, such as feeding, treats, security, and sleep. To maximize the crate training process:

• Make the crate attractive to your puppy by placing an old blanket, towel or rug and a few of his favorite indestructible chew toys inside the crate. Remember, young puppies love to chew so choose toys and blankets that are safe and do not present a potential choking hazard.

• Leave the crate door open and allow your puppy to explore in and around the crate. If your puppy goes inside the crate, praise him. "Good puppy!" or "Aren't you clever!" Reward him with a tasty tidbit while he is in the crate.

• If your puppy is reluctant to go inside, encourage him by letting him see you toss a tasty tidbit of food inside the crate, preferably toward the back of the crate. When your puppy goes inside the crate to retrieve the food, praise him. "Good puppy!"

Benefits of Crate Usage

A key to successful puppy rearing is to never put your puppy in a position where he can get himself into trouble. Any puppy left unsupervised will develop bad habits. In record time, your adorable Border Collie puppy can pee from one end of the house to the other, ransack the trash, and gnaw the leg off your dining room chair. Does the expression, "I just turned my back for a second!" sound familiar? During those short periods when you cannot watch your puppy closely, a crate prevents him from getting into mischief.

A crate is one of the safest, most successful, and efficient ways to housetrain a young puppy, or adult dog. If your Border Collie has an accident in his crate, the mess is much easier to clean and less damaging when it is not in the middle of your Persian rug.

A crate is also ideal for keeping your Border Collie safe while traveling. A crated dog will not distract you from your driving responsibilities, teethe on your leather armrests, try to snatch French fries from the cashier at the drive-up window, or eat your cell phone. Many motels and hotels, as well as friends and family, are more receptive to dogs provided they are crate trained. As your Border Collie grows and matures, the crate will continue to be his den and safe place for eating, sleeping, and retreating from the often chaotic and noisy world of humans.

- Feed your puppy his meals inside the crate, luring him inside with his food bowl. This makes the crate a positive place for your puppy to be.
- When your puppy is comfortable being inside the crate and shows no signs of stress, try closing the door for one minute. Do not latch the door. Open the door and praise your puppy for being brave. "Look at you! You're so brave!"
- As your puppy becomes more comfortable with the crate, you can gradually increase the time that he spends there. Never confine him for longer than one hour at a time—except at night when he is sleeping.

A dog who is crate trained can be brought along almost anywhere and have a safe and secure refuge.

- If your puppy whines or cries, avoid reinforcing the behavior by letting him out the crate or coddling him, such as saying, "What's the matter, honey?" Wait for him to be quiet for a minute or two before opening the door (provided you are certain he does not need to relieve himself).
- If you are working and cannot let your puppy out every hour— employ a reliable relative, friend, or neighbor to exercise your puppy during the day. Or, try using a playpen or exercise pen. This will give your puppy room to play, exercise, and relieve himself if necessary.

HOUSETRAINING

The object of housetraining is to teach your puppy to relieve himself outdoors and not on your Oriental rug, in the corner of the living room, or all over the house. Housetraining is a relatively easy and painless process, yet it often causes owners a great deal of anxiety. Good planning and preparation and your unwavering commitment to the situation will provide your puppy with the best possible start. Crate training, when done properly, helps quickly and efficiently housetrain a puppy.

As a general rule, Border Collies are no more difficult to housetrain than any other breed. Some puppies can be more difficult to housetrain than others, but that has more to do with

If you see this little face staring up at you in the middle of the night, someone probably needs to go!

the individual puppy, rather than a reflection of the breed. The key to successful housetraining is vigilance and consistency on the part of the owner.

If your puppy was born in the wild, he would live in a cave or den, and most den animals have an inherent desire to keep their dens clean. As a result, they instinctively will try not to eliminate in their den. A crate serves as your puppy's den. If you watch a litter of puppies, you will notice around three weeks of age the puppies will instinctively begin moving away from the whelping box in order to relieve themselves. This deep-seated denning instinct and an innate tendency to keep the den clean provide the foundation of housetraining via use of a crate. If you take advantage of this instinct, you reduce the chance of accidents. As your puppy matures, you gradually teach him to hold his bladder for longer periods of time.

To increase your chances of success while minimizing accidents, you will need to provide your puppy with a regular schedule of eating, sleeping, and eliminating. Dogs are creatures of habit, and they will have an easier time adjusting to their new household and a housetraining schedule if you provide some order and routine to their lives.

It is worth noting that these steps works equally well when housetraining an adult dog—especially if you have acquired a rescue or shelter dog. In these instances, it is always best to assume he is not housetrained and begin the housetraining process from step one.

Understand Your Puppy for Housetraining Success

The first step in any successful housetraining program is recognizing that young puppies have very little or no bladder control until around five months of age. Puppies mature at different rates so your puppy's control may develop earlier or later. A seven- to eight-week-old puppy is equivalent to a four- to six-month-old human baby. You would not expect a young baby to control his bladder, and it is unfair to ask your puppy to exercise control that he does not have.

Puppies are most active during the day—running, jumping, training, playing, exploring, and being a puppy. Because of their limited bladder size and lack of control, it goes without saying that they are going to need to relieve themselves many, many times throughout the day. During the night, however, puppies are usually exhausted from their busy day of being a puppy. They are more relaxed and as a result most puppies can sleep between five and eight hours without having to potty. This varies from puppy to puppy, and in this sense they are not unlike human babies. Some parents get lucky and their babies sleep through the night. Others are relegated to months of sleeplessness.

If you have a puppy that wakes you up in the middle of the night or the early morning when he feels the need to go, it is best to get up with him rather than allow him to have an accident in his crate. While it may seem like forever, it will not be long before he can hold on all night.

How to Housetrain Your Border Collie

First thing each morning when you hear that unmistakable whimper, let your puppy out of his crate and immediately take him outdoors to a designated spot. Do not dawdle or allow yourself to get sidetracked making coffee, checking your e-mail, or fumbling around for a leash—keep one in a convenient spot. A few seemingly insignificant minutes to you is long enough to guarantee an accident for your puppy. Remember, your puppy been confined in his crate for several hours, and he just can't wait another two or three minutes. He needs to go right now!

While you are outside, watch your puppy to make sure he empties his bladder or bowels. It may take a few minutes, so be patient. When your puppy has finished doing his business, calmly praise: "Good puppy!" or "Good pee!" Once you have seen your puppy relieve himself outdoors, you can allow him supervised play indoors. If you take your puppy outdoors and he does not relieve himself, it is important that you

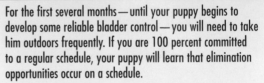

When to Take Your Puppy to Potty

For the first several months—until your puppy begins to develop some reliable bladder control—you will need to take him outdoors frequently. If you are 100 percent committed to a regular schedule, your puppy will learn that elimination opportunities occur on a schedule.

As a general guideline—to increase your chances of success while minimizing accidents—take your puppy outdoors at the following times:

- First thing in the morning when he wakes up.
- About 15 minutes after drinking water.
- About 30 minutes after eating.
- Immediately after waking from a nap.
- First thing when you arrive home.
- At least once every hour during the day.
- Last thing at night.

This guideline is for young puppies. Because puppies are individuals and must be treated as such, you may need to tweak or adjust this schedule to fit your puppy's individual needs. No one said raising a puppy was all fun and no work! Housetraining a puppy is a time-consuming endeavor, but time invested at this stage will make your life easier in the long run.

put him back in his crate for five or ten minutes and then repeat the aforementioned steps. (If you are not using a crate to housetrain, you will need to keep your puppy where you can watch him for those five or ten minutes.) Do this as many times as necessary until your puppy relieves himself. Do not assume your puppy has done his business. Seeing is believing, and you need to see your puppy empty his bladder or bowels. You will need to repeat this routine many, many times throughout the day and again just before you go to bed at night.

Your Role

Why go to all this trouble? The importance of going with your puppy and watching him has many important purposes. First, if your puppy is on leash, you can take him to the same spot each time he needs to eliminate. This helps establish the habit of using a certain area of your yard. This also helps to keep your puppy on track and prevent him from getting too distracted with the potpourri of sights, smells, and sounds. Puppies are naturally curious and easily distracted. While sniffing the ground usually helps to speed up the process, if your puppy gets too distracted and forgets to go—when you bring him back indoors and he is no longer distracted, he will feel a sudden urge to go and it is highly likely that he will go on your carpet.

Puppies who are raised on a schedule and with clear expectations about house rules will soon master housetraining.

Young puppies, generally under the age of three months, find comfort and security by being close to you. If you leave while your puppy is searching for a spot to potty, he will most likely run after you and forget about the task at hand. If you put him outdoors and leave him to his own devices, it is highly likely he will spend most of his time trying to get back in the house to be with you, and again, he will have forgotten his mission. In addition, by going outside with your puppy, you can praise him for doing what you want which is going to the bathroom outdoors. Praise will help your puppy to understand exactly what you want and that will maximize the learning process.

Learning to Interpret the Signals

Where owners often run afoul is by thinking their puppy is housetrained when it is really only wishful thinking on their part. Puppies between the ages of eight and ten weeks do not show signs of having to urinate. When they have to go, they go right away—often stopping to urinate in the middle of a play session. It is unrealistic to expect your puppy to stop what he is doing and tell you when he needs to go outside. More often than not, your puppy will not realize he has to go until he is already going. Your job for the next six months, or longer depending on the puppy, is to keep an eye on your puppy and anticipate his bathroom needs.

Around 10 or 12 weeks of age, a puppy will start to exhibit signs—warning signals that he is about to urinate or defecate—by circling, making crying noises, sniffing the floor or arching his back. Oftentimes, his tail will come up or he might stand by the door. This is where owners get over-confident and think they are home free. These are signs that your puppy is learning, not that he is housetrained. Now more than ever you need to remain diligent and stick to the program. You can begin teaching him which signal to use to let you know he needs to go outside by reinforcing any or all of the signals.

By following these simple steps, your puppy will learn through repetition and consistency to relieve himself outdoors. Patience and consistency are the keys to housetraining. There are no short cuts. You mustn't become complacent. You will only be creating problems that will exist for many years to come. The more your puppy can do his business outdoors, the quicker he will learn, the happier you will be, and the sooner the entire family can get back to being barefoot in the house!

Accidents Will Happen

While it is in yours and your dog's best interest to keep indoor accidents to a minimum, few owners escape puppy rearing without an accident here or there. If an accident does happen, consider it your fault and be more observant in the future. Never scold or hit

Eliminating on Cue

By accompanying your puppy, you can also begin instilling a verbal cue for the command, such as "Go pee" or "Go potty." A notable English trainer likes to use the cue "Go wee!" You can choose a separate word for urinating and defecating. Whatever cue words you choose, be sure they are words you will be comfortable using for many years and in front of neighbors, visitors, and in-laws. These verbal cues should be given each time your puppy is in the process of urinating or defecating, otherwise you will teach him the wrong association. The words should be said in a calm but encouraging tone of voice. If your voice is too excitable, your puppy will most likely forget what he is doing and run to see what you are so excited about.

your puppy and never, ever rub his nose in the mess. Those are not housetraining techniques—they are crimes in progress. Punishing, yelling, or otherwise berating your puppy will only confuse him and prolong the housetraining process.

Dogs live in the moment. Young or old, they do not have the mental wherewithal to associate the punishment they are receiving with an earlier act of urinating on the floor. When you scold or tell

Don't be too hard on your puppy if he has an accident. He may try to hide his mistakes to avoid your anger.

off your puppy, he will display a submissive response. Your puppy is reacting to your mannerisms and tone of voice. Most owners tend to misinterpret their puppy's submissive demeanor as comprehension that he did something wrong. They often say, "He knows what he did wrong. He even looks guilty!"

Furthermore, scolding, punishing or berating your puppy is counterproductive to building a solid, trusting, and mutually respectful relationship. A puppy who lives in fear of you is likely to grow into an adult dog that is anxious and frequently worried. If he potties on the floor and you scold him when you get home ten minutes or two hours later, it is highly likely that he will become anxious and perhaps fearful of being left alone, which can exacerbate urinating in the house or cause him to develop all sorts of unwanted behaviors as he grows into an adult dog.

What To Do at Night

If your puppy wakes you up when he feels the need to go and you find you simply cannot get up several times during the night—you can cover an area of the floor with sheets of newspaper. This works particularly well in a kitchen, which is usually vinyl or linoleum. Set up an exercise pen on top of the newspaper and put his crate inside the exercise pen. At night, leave his crate door open. He will have access to his crate for sleeping, and he can also potty on the paper if he needs to go. The exercise pen will keep him confined to a small area.

This technique works in a pinch. However, it is worth noting that it is always worthwhile to make the effort to get up with your puppy if he needs to go outside, as teaching your puppy to urinate on newspaper can create its own set of problems. Puppies who learn to urinate in the house—even on newspaper—have learned it is okay to urinate in the house. It's not their fault. It's what you have inadvertently taught him. This can be a difficult habit to break the older he gets, and then teaching him to reliably relieve himself outdoors becomes more difficult.

TRAINING YOUR BORDER COLLIE

Puppies and adult dogs learn through repetition and consistency. To provide your puppy with a basic foundation of obedience skills and manners that allow him to grow into a well-behaved adult dog and co-exist with humans, you must be consistent with your expectations. Dogs learn faster when the rules stay the same.

It is very important that your dog trusts you and does not feel he must worry about how you are going to react from day to day. For instance, it is unfair to allow an eight-week-old puppy to jump on you today, but scold him for doing so tomorrow when his feet are muddy. He does not have the mental capacity to understand his feet are muddy and your white silk pants are expensive. If you do not want your adult Border Collie jumping on you—you should discourage the behavior from day one when he is a young, impressionable puppy. It is unfair to allow your adorable puppy on the furniture today, but reprimand him for the same behavior when he is a 50-pound (22.5 kilogram) adult dog. It is unfair to feed your dog at the table every night, then act mortified and correct him when he begs your in-laws for tidbits of steak and potatoes. Think ahead, and decide which behaviors you will or will not accept and which behaviors you can or cannot live with for the next 12 to 15 years.

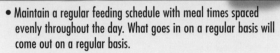

Housetraining Tips

• Maintain a regular feeding schedule with meal times spaced evenly throughout the day. What goes in on a regular basis will come out on a regular basis.

• As a general rule, puppies need to relieve themselves about 15 to 20 minutes after drinking water and 30 minutes after eating.

• Make a mental note of the size, shape, and color of your puppy's stools. When you know what is normal, you'll know when something is amiss.

• Limit your puppy's food and water intake approximately one hour before you turn out the lights. This will help to insure his bladder and bowels are empty. Note: do not restrict water intake during the day, but do avoid allowing your puppy to drink heavily as bedtime approaches.

• Choose a quality food designed for your puppy's needs and try to stick with it, provided there are no problems. Avoid changing brands from week to week, especially during the housetraining phase. Changing foods can upset your puppy's digestive tract and complicate the housetraining process. If you must change foods, do it gradually.

• Cheaper foods are not always the best buy. Premium foods cost more, but they are usually more digestible, often resulting in smaller stool.

• Feed the same amount of food at each feeding. Pick up any uneaten food after 15 minutes. This keeps your puppy's digestive tract on a regular schedule and helps to prevent finicky eaters.

• Avoid free-feeding—putting your puppy's food bowl on the floor and allowing him to nibble throughout the day, at his leisure.

• Despite what your close friends and in-laws say, most puppies are not thoroughly and reliably housetrained until they are seven or eight months of age—some even a year old.

When Accidents Mean Something Else

Accidents are bound to happen during the housetraining process, but some breeds are more challenging than others. Small breeds, submissive or stressed puppies, and heavily kenneled puppies, can be especially challenging. You should seek veterinary assistance if you observe any of the following conditions:

• Change in color or odor of urine

• Change in frequency of urination

• Sudden change in the number of accidents

• Sweet or foul odor to the puppy

Understanding the Individual

Equally important in the training process is understanding that all puppies are individuals. A litter of Border Collie puppies may look alike, but they have their own unique character, temperament, and personality. As a result of their genetic make-up, plus some environmental influences, they will grow into adult dogs who possess their own distinct qualities.

If you have children, think how each was raised with the same amount of love, individual attention, rules, values, and so forth in order to make the most of their personality and talents. Yet despite a seemingly uniform upbringing, each child is an individual with his or her own special talents, likes, dislikes, quirks, and idiosyncrasies.

This is where a keen understanding of the Border Collie breed—his history and origin—will help you to better understand what makes your puppy tick. Get in the habit of watching your puppy when he is sleeping, playing by himself, or with other animals or with children. Is he bold? Sassy? Pushy? Bossy? Does he cower from the children? Does he growl or attack other dogs or cats in the household? Is he inquisitive? Does he have ants in his pants?

Understanding your puppy's individual personality will help you to recognize which behaviors you can live with and those that might preclude a long and happy human / canine relationship. If, for instance, your puppy is bossy and pushy, you will want to begin right away discouraging the behavior of bolting outdoors or grabbing food or toys from your hand without permission. If your puppy is a bit shy and nervous, you will want to expose him to safe situations that will help build his confidence, such as encouraging friends to get on the ground and talk to him, play with him, rub his tummy, and kiss his nose. You will want to take him for rides in the car, to the veterinarian's for a cookie and a kiss, or trips to the neighbor's barn—on leash, of course—to see the horses and explore strange smells, sights, and sounds.

Types of Training

Many wonderful methods are available for training puppies and adult dogs. The hardest part is deciphering the enormous variety of training methods and trainers. What works, what doesn't? Who's right, who's wrong? In today's canine-friendly environment, it seems there are as many trainers and training methods as there are breeds of dogs. Positive and negative motivation, food training, play training, toy training, and clicker training—throw in the endless variety of paraphernalia employed—from electronic gizmos to metallic gadgetry—and the entire process can seem more complicated than computer science.

The good news is that Border Collies are highly trainable and quick to learn, and raising and training a Border Collie is not terribly difficult. It is well within the capabilities of most dog owners who set their minds to it. It does, however, require time, insight, dedication, and the ability to view setbacks with a sense of humor. Most Border Collies love to work for and please their owners, but they do not like to be bullied. They must be trained and handled with respect, fairness, and consistency.

A key ingredient to successful dog training is having a clear picture of what you want to accomplish and a well thought out game plan, which includes regular training, socialization, and interaction with your puppy both at home and in public. Additionally, it helps if you start right away—preferably as soon as your Border Collie starts living with you.

Years ago, the accepted methodology of dog training was that a puppy had to be at least six months old before you began teaching basic obedience skills. That concept has since been debunked and modern-day breeders, trainers, and animal behaviorists now recognize the important benefits of early training—as early as eight weeks of age. Additionally, trainers from the past often employed the standard *pop and jerk* type training that involved a choke chain, force, and a total domination of the dog. While that method usually produced desired results it often came at a hefty price that included stifling a dog's madcap personality, as well as his willingness and desire to please. Many of those methods produced dogs who obeyed commands out of fear rather than a desire to please their owners.

Today's top trainers had the foresight and willingness to change by recognizing the

Just like people, Border Collies are each unique, with their own rates of learning and ability.

Keep it Fun!

Regardless of whether you call it formal or informal training, you can maximize your dog's training by avoiding techniques that are repetitious, predictable, and boring for him. Border Collies are intelligent, quick to learn, and always ready for a game. As a result, they can also become bored quite quickly, too. Therefore, you will need to use your imagination to be creative and come up with fun training techniques and games that stimulate your Border Collie's mind and increase his desire to learn.

Dogs are naturally curious and love to explore and test their boundaries. Therefore, it is best to begin your dog's training in a familiar environment with a limited amount of distractions, such as your house or yard. This is especially helpful if you are training a young puppy.

importance of allowing dogs and handlers to be themselves, rather than imposing the same training method regardless of temperament. While you can still find trainers that adhere to the ideology of force and domination as a means of training, most trainers today employ gentler training methods that include praise, positive motivation, and positive reinforcement.

The concept behind positive motivation/ reinforcement is that a favorable consequence to a behavior encourages repetition of that behavior. A dog learns to repeat a behavior, such as sit, down, or come, in order to receive a reward. The reward can be a combination of verbal or physical praise coupled with a tasty tidbit of food or his favorite toy.

Formal or Informal Training?

Owning a Border Collie, or any dog for that matter, should be fun. Otherwise, what is the point? The same concept of fun should apply to training and playing. The goal is to teach your dog to cheerfully and eagerly respond to a variety of commands both on and off leash and under a range of circumstances, such as in your yard, at the park, and even when he is playing with his canine buddies. Owners often run amok by getting caught up in too much formal training and not enough fun, informal training. The primary difference between formal and informal training is the degree of precision. Formal training, however, does not mean all work and no play. It should be equally as fun as informal training.

Few owners are going to require their Border Collie to respond with the precision of top-ranked obedience competitors. Nor are they necessarily interested in whether or not their dog sits perfectly straight, or if he took an extra step before he responded to the down command. While these are matters of utmost concern to competitive trainers, most Border Collie owners are quite happy when their dog sits on command or comes when he is called.

Puppy Kindergarten

If your Border Collie is between two and five months of age, a puppy kindergarten class is an ideal environment for exposing and socializing him to everything he will encounter in his adult life, such as other dogs, kids, stairways, strange noises and smells, trashcans, women in floppy hats, and so forth. Puppy classes will help your Border Collie continue to expand on his knowledge of canine communication and social skills that he learned from his canine mother and while interacting with his littermates. As he grows and matures, he will learn to communicate and interact with other dogs in a low-risk and stress-free environment.

Puppy classes should not be a free-for-all where puppies play

Border Collies work best when they're enjoying the experience. Keep training fun and end every session on a high note.

No License Required

Dog training is a self-regulating profession. Anyone can call themselves a behaviorist, consultant, or trainer. They are not required to be licensed, and there are no governing agencies to regulate training techniques and devices that may be cruel or inhumane. As the guardian of your dog's well being, it is up to you to protect him by educating yourself and selecting the person best qualified to work with your dog. A word of caution—it is not always the most expensive trainer or behaviorist!

on their own while their owners socialize on the sidelines. A well-structured puppy class will include teaching basic obedience skills including fun puppy recall games, sit, down, and name recognition. You will learn how to read canine body language, how to train your puppy, and how to recognize problems early on before they become annoying, ingrained habits that are difficult to break.

Finding a Trainer

To find the right trainer or puppy class for you and your Border Collie:
- Ask your veterinarian, breeder, dog groomer, or dog-owning friends for referrals. Word of mouth is a great tool for uncovering talented and knowledgeable trainers, while avoiding problem ones.
- Contact professional organizations that certify or recommend trainers, such as the Association of Pet Dog Trainers or National Association of Dog Obedience Instructors.
- Attend the classes of several trainers to observe their personalities, training techniques, and facilities.
- Look for trainers who focus on rewarding what your puppy does right rather than punishing what he does wrong.
- Does the trainer recognize that puppies are individuals? Are the same training methods imposed on all the puppies regardless of their mental maturity?
- Puppies learn best in low-risk, stress-free environments. Look for classes that are structured, run smoothly, yet still emphasize fun.
- Do the facilities provide a safe learning environment for you and your puppy? Are they well lit with matted floors and eight to ten puppies per class?
- Are the puppies separated—small puppies from large, young puppies from juniors, the rambunctious from the shy?
- Trust your instinct. Your puppy's safety and well-being are paramount. If you feel uncomfortable about the facility or trainer, find another puppy class.

Basic Obedience

The object of teaching basic obedience skills is to provide your Border Collie with a set of commands he understands, thereby making your life and his more enjoyable. Trying to physically restrain a 50-pound (22.5 kilogram) Border Collie who wants to zig when you want to zag is enough to make you wish you had bought a cat. A Border Collie without a solid foundation of canine manners and obedience skills can quickly grow into an unruly hooligan. A Border Collie who is taught to respond reliably and quickly to basic commands is much easier and enjoyable to live with. No doubt, his life is more pleasurable because, as a well-behaved dog, he is more likely to be incorporated into the family environment rather than relegated to the isolation of the backyard.

TEACHING THE COMMANDS

The first step in teaching any exercise is to have a clear picture in your mind of what you want to teach. If you are teaching your Border Collie to sit, have a clear picture in your mind of what a sit looks like. This may seem simple, if not downright silly, but if you cannot visualize it in your mind, how can you teach it, and more importantly, how can your dog learn it? Many owners have different ideas of what a sit or a down or even a come command represent. Some owners are happy if their dog comes on the eight or ninth command. Others want their Border Collie to come the first time he is called. The choice is yours. Puppies have limited attention spans and are easily distracted by kids playing, toys lying around, birds flying overhead, a bug on the ground, cows mooing, horses whinnying, and so forth. It is unreasonable to expect a young puppy to ignore all the distractions and focus entirely on you. "It's a bit like taking a child to Disneyland for the first time and expecting it to learn logarithms," says Annette Conn, English dog trainer and author of the book, *It's a Dog's Life*.

Therefore, it is best to begin your dog's training in a familiar environment that has a limited amount of distractions, such as your house or yard.

Sit

Sit is one of those must-know commands for every dog. A dog who understands the sit command provides you with an avenue of control. Think of the many situations when your Border Collie will need to know how to sit—at the vet's office, waiting to

Tips for Successful Dog Training

- Puppies and young dogs have limited attention spans. Keep sessions short: train two or three times a day, five or ten minutes per session.

- Training must always be fun. Fun games maximize your dog's propensity to learn.

Train when your dog is awake and eager to play. Never wake up your dog in order to train.

- Dogs learn at different rates. Train within your dog's mental and physical capabilities. Never progress at a speed faster than your dog's ability to comprehend.

- Set achievable goals to keep you and your puppy motivated. Keep training steps small, and praise your dog every time he does a tiny step right.

- Always use a command when you use your dog's name. "Fido, come!" or "Fido, down." If you repeatedly say your dog's name without putting a command with it, it is a form of nagging and eventually your dog will become desensitized to his name.

- Always end a play/training session on a positive note.

- Get in the habit of saying the command one time. Avoid repeating yourself: "Sit, sit, sit, %#$@! SIT!" If you say it ten times, your Border Collie will wait until the tenth command to respond.

- Make sure you give your puppy the release word before you allow him to rise out of the sit position. Doing so will clearly signal to the puppy the end of the exercise.

- Avoid saying, "Sit down" when you really mean "Sit."

be fed, waiting to cross the street, or sitting while you open any door. He will need to sit when you put his collar on or take it off, when you want to check his coat for stickers or burrs, or when you want to brush him or trim his nails. The sit command increases his vocabulary and instills order in both of your lives! Teaching the sit command is relatively simple, and the guidelines are the same whether you are teaching a young puppy or an adult dog.

1. Begin with your puppy on leash. This is especially helpful if your dog, like most puppies, has his own agenda, tends to wander off, or is easily distracted.

2. Start with your leash in one hand, a tasty tidbit in the other hand, and your puppy standing in front of you. (Hold the tidbit firmly between your thumb and index finger so your dog cannot get it until he is in the correct position.)

3. Show your puppy the tidbit by holding it close to and slightly above his nose. As your puppy raises his nose to take the food, slowly move the cookie in a slightly upward and backward direction toward his tail, keeping the cookie directly above his nose. (If your puppy jumps up or brings his front feet off the ground, the cookie is too high. If he walks backwards, the cookie is too far back or too low.)

4. At this point, your puppy's hips should automatically sink toward the ground. As they do, give the sit command. While your puppy is sitting, praise him with "Good sit!" and reward him with the tidbit. (Give the sit command as your puppy's rear end hits the ground. Saying it too soon will teach the wrong association.)

5. Release your puppy with a release word, such as "free" or "okay," play with him for a few seconds and repeat the exercise three or four times in succession, three or four times a day.

Down

"Down" is an equally important and useful command. You can use the down command when you are watching television, sewing, preparing dinner, reading quietly, or when friends come to visit and you do not want your dog directly involved in what you are doing at that moment. Your dog may need to lie down on the vet's exam table, while you brush or scratch his tummy, check his coat for stickers, or when you want to massage his sore muscles. Teaching the down command can be a bit more challenging than the sit, as it is considered a submissive position for some dogs. If

your puppy has an independent personality, this exercise will take a bit more patience and persistence on your part. Do not give up! Remember, puppies learn through repetition and consistency.

1. Begin by kneeling on the floor so you are eye level with your puppy.

2. With your puppy standing in front of you, hold a tasty tidbit of food in one hand; place your other hand in his buckle collar under his chin with your fingertips pointing down.

3. Let your puppy sniff the cookie. Simultaneously, move the cookie toward the floor between his front feet while you apply gentle downward and backward pressure with your hand that is in the collar.

4. When done correctly, your puppy will plant his front feet and fold his body into the down position as he follows the cookie to the ground.

5. When his elbows and tummy are on the ground, give the command, "Down."

6. While your puppy is in the down position, reward with the cookie and *calmly* praise, "Good down."

7. Release your puppy with a release word, such as "free" or "okay," repeat the exercise three or four times in succession, three or four times a day.

Stay

The goal is to teach your dog to stay in a specific position, such as in a "sit" or "down," until you say it is okay to move. It is useful in a variety of situations, such as when you want to answer or open the door without your Border Collie bolting through it. To teach sit-stay:

- Start with your puppy on a loose leash, sitting beside you. Tell your puppy to sit and to stay. You can include a hand signal by holding the open palm of your hand in front of your puppy's face about two inches from his nose as you say "Stay".

- Watch your dog closely for the slightest movement that may indicate he is about to stand up or lie down. Try to be proactive in your training by reminding your dog to stay *before* he moves.

- Once he has remained in position for a few seconds, praise calmly and warmly with "Good stay" and a tidbit of cookie. You can include calm, physical praise, such as gentle stroking—but not so enthusiastically that he gets excited and forgets the task at hand.

- As soon as you see any movement, repeat your stay command

Tips for Training "Down"

- If your puppy resists your hand in the collar: follow the above instructions but rather than putting your hand in the collar—apply light pressure with the flat of your hand on your Border Collie's shoulder blades. Don't push too hard or force the issue. Doing so can injure your puppy.

- Avoid sliding your hand down his back: you may put pressure on the wrong spot and hurt him.

- If your puppy resists, avoid getting into a wrestling match with him. Simply abort the exercise and try again.

- Make sure you give your puppy a release word before you allow him to rise out of the down position. Doing so will clearly signal to the dog the end of the exercise.

- Get in the habit of saying the command one time. Avoid repeating yourself: "Down, down, down, I said DOWN!"

- Be careful not to use the command "Sit down" when you really mean "Down."

- Avoid confusing your dog by using the down command when you really mean "off"—such as getting off the furniture or not jumping on you.

firmly, but not harshly.

- If your dog stands up, use your leash to prevent him from moving away and get him into the sit position again. If he lies down, gently reposition him and remind him to stay.

- Reward him with a cookie first and then release him with an "okay" or "free" command. (If you release your dog first and then reward him, you will teach him the wrong association. He will think he is being rewarded for moving. This can teach a puppy to anticipate the reward, thereby encouraging him to break the stay command.)

- As your puppy matures and can remain sitting beside you for two or three minutes without moving, you can progress by giving the stay command and then stepping directly in front of his nose. Gradually begin increasing the distance between you and your puppy.

Tips for Teaching "Stay"

- Many puppies are not emotionally mature enough to cope with this exercise until they are five or six months old. If this is the case with your puppy, do not force the issue. Simply wait until he is older and mentally more mature to understand and cope with the exercise.

- When first learning this command, five or ten seconds in the stay position is long enough for most dogs.

- Gradually, over a number of sessions and in five-second increments, increase the time your Border Collie remains in position.

- Do not be in a hurry to move away from your dog or have him hold the position for longer periods.

- Young puppies have limited attention spans. How fast your Border Collie progresses with this exercise will depend on his mental maturity.

- Do not nag, scold, or send him threatening looks during a stay. Dogs who are bullied or intimidated into staying are less reliable in the long run. Dogs learn faster and retain more information when they learn in a stress-free environment.

- Never leave your dog in a stay position unsupervised, such as outside a store or anywhere he could run off, be hurt, stolen, or lost.

- Avoid using the stay command when you really mean "wait," such as, "Wait in the yard," or "Wait in the car until I get back."

- Once you have a reliable sit-stay in a non-distractive situation, you can begin incorporating mild distractions, such as toys lying nearby on the floor. As your dog becomes reliable with mild distractions, you can begin escalating the distractions. Try training while other people or dogs play nearby. If your dog has a difficult time focusing on the task at hand, perhaps the increase in distractions was too soon or severe.

- To teach the down-stay, begin with your dog in the down position, and tell him to stay. Then follow the remaining instructions for the sit-stay. Avoid teaching the sit-stay and down-stay in succession. This will confuse your puppy. Practice the sit-stay one day, and the down-stay another day.

Come

The goal is to teach your puppy to come to you reliably, willingly, and immediately—without hesitation—upon hearing the command, while in a wide range of situations, such as at the park, in the neighbor's yard, at a friend's house, in an emergency, or anytime he gets loose. *Immediately* in your dog's mind should never mean, "OK I hear you. I'll be there as soon as I finish chasing this bug." You want your dog to understand that when you say "Come!" it means, "Stop what you are doing and run back to me as fast as you can—right now." In the beginning, you teach this behavior with fun games and tasty rewards. Ideally, as he grows into an adult dog, you want him to come to you because he *wants* to be with you—not just because you have a cookie. This is why it is so important to connect with him mentally—to establish a strong bond and human/canine relationship.

Coming when called should never mean playtime is over. When you call your puppy, you should do something silly with him when he gets to you, such as a quick game of tug, a fun trick, or reward him with a tasty tidbit, and then let him run off and play again. Where owners often run afoul is by calling their puppy only when it is time to go in his kennel or to put his leash on and go home. In these situations, your puppy will quickly learn that "come" means the end of his freedom, and he is likely to avoid you the next time he is called.

When teaching the come command, you should call your puppy only when you are absolutely certain he will respond. For example, if you call your puppy when he is excited about greeting another dog, when a family member has just come to visit, or when he is eating his dinner, he will be too excited and distracted to respond to your command, and you will inadvertently be teaching him to ignore you. In the early stages, when your puppy is learning the come command, it is prudent to wait until the excitement has subsided and then call him to you. If you must have your puppy during these times, it is better to go and get him rather than call him to you.

Equally important, take advantage of opportunities where you can set him up to succeed by calling him back to you when he would be coming to you anyway, such as when you have just arrived home and he is running toward you, or when you have his dinner or a tasty tidbit. Let him know how clever he is when he gets to you.

A puppy who views come as a fun game is more likely to develop a reliable response to the come command. If this behavior continues throughout his puppyhood, and you remain excited and enthusiastic

each and every time he comes to you, you will have a strong and positive response to the behavior as he grows and matures into an adult dog.

Your can use an informal game like "find me!" to begin teaching "come" in a positive, fun, and exciting manner. This game capitalizes on a dog's natural chase instinct. It is also an excellent game for instilling the come command in your puppies.

• Start with a pocket full of tasty tidbits.

• Rev your puppy up by showing him a yummy treat and then toss the treat down the hallway or across the living room.

• As your puppy runs for the cookie, you run in the opposite direction and hide behind a chair or door as you say his name enthusiastically.

• When your puppy finds you, make a big fuss: get on the floor, roll around, and lavish him with a potpourri of kisses and praise. "Good Come!" or "You found me!"

• Repeat the game several times throughout the day, but not so many times that your dog becomes bored.

• You can also play this game outdoors. Be sure to play in a fenced area to protect your dog from harm or prevent him from running off. When you are outside in your garden or yard with your dog and he stops to sniff the grass or explore a bug—duck behind a tree or bush, clap your hands and say his name in an excited tone of voice.

• When your dog gets to you, greet him with plenty of hugs, kisses, and praise, "Good Come!" or "Good boy!" It is not necessary for your dog to sit before he gets a treat. If you insist on your puppy sitting first, you will not be rewarding the most important part of the exercise, which is coming to you.

• Anytime he voluntarily comes back to you—without you asking him to—praise him, "Good come!" and reward him with a tasty tidbit. He will quickly learn that being with you is fun—and rewarding!

LEASH TRAINING

Walking a 45-pound Border Collie that wants to zig when you want to zag is a frustrating challenge for even the most patient (and strongest!) owners. There are several variations to walking on leash. The formal heel command is used by most obedience competitors who are sticklers for precision. They spend years teaching their dogs to walk with their heads and bodies in a specific position. Most Border Collie owners are not going to require that much precision. They are quite happy if their dogs are not dragging them down the street.

While the traditional heel position is on the handler's left side, there may be times when you do not care if he is on your left side, right side, or walking out in front of you. That said, it is always easier to teach your puppy to walk on leash by starting on the left side and sticking with it until he understands the exercise. Once he has mastered walking nicely on leash, you can allow him to walk on the right side or out in front of you.

Getting Started With Very Young Puppies

It is important that your puppy not associate his leash and collar

Once your Border Collie has learned what "down" means, you can use a hand signal to get him in position.

with a barrage of corrections or nagging. He should view walking beside you as something fun that he does with his mom.

To begin:

1. Always teach this exercise on a buckle collar, never a choke-chain Young puppies rarely, if ever, need a choke chain for training. It's too harsh. You aren't correcting the puppy. You are managing his behaviors. Plus, when a puppy or adult dog drags a leash or long-line attached to a choke chain, the leash can get snagged on a bush, tree, fence post, etc., and inadvertently choke the puppy.

2. Attach a leash (or thin long-line) to his collar and allow him to drag it around. Don't worry if he picks it up and tries to carry it around. In fact, put a command to the behavior. "Have you got your leash?" eventually becomes "Get your leash!"

3. When your puppy is happily dragging the leash, pick it up and start walking forward, encouraging your puppy to walk close to your left side by talking sweetly to him and luring him with a tasty tidbit from your left hand. (This is easier if the leash is in your right hand.)

4. When you have walked a few steps with your dog on your left side, reward him with the tidbit of food. Remember to verbally praise and offer the food reward when he is close beside your left leg. This will encourage him to remain in position.

5. Once your puppy is comfortable walking beside you, you can begin teaching a more formal "walk nicely on leash."

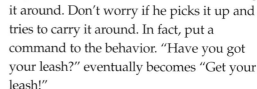

Tips for Teaching "Come"

- Your dog must always chase you. Avoid making a game of you chasing your dog, and never allow kids to chase your dog. It inadvertently teaches him to run away from you, which creates problems down the road.

- If you want a dog that reliably comes to you when he is called, the come command must always be positive.

- If your puppy comes to you, you must always, always, always praise him—even if moments before he chewed your shoes, urinated on the floor, or ransacked the trash. There are no exceptions to this rule.

- Never call your dog to come and then correct him for something he did, such as chewing your shoe or urinating on the floor. Punishing him when he gets to you will only make it less likely that he will come back the next time. If you want to correct your dog, go and get him. Do not call him to you.

- Do not call your dog to come if you want to give him a bath, administer medications, or anything else he might find unpleasant. Instead, go and get your dog and then put him in the tub, trim his nails, administer medications, etc.

- Never allow your puppy to run off leash in an unfenced or unconfined area. Doing so puts your puppy at risk and teaches him bad habits because he is too young to reliably respond to the come command.

- Once your puppy develops a reliable response to the come command—meaning he comes each and every time he is called—you can begin teaching this exercise in more distracting circumstances.

Walk Nicely on Leash

The goal is to teach your puppy to walk nicely on leash—anywhere within the full extension of his leash, on either side of you or in front of you—without pulling. He should also learn that a loose leash means he goes forward. Highly rewarding! Pulling on the leash means he stops. Definitely non-

rewarding! Puppies who learn not to yank their owner's shoulder out of the socket grow into adult dogs who do not pull on their leashes. They are a joy to own because it is fun to take them for walks, and they are more likely to be included in family outings. To begin:

- Teach this exercise on a buckle collar, never on a choke chain.
- With your puppy on leash, encourage him to stand close to your left leg by luring him into position with a tasty tidbit of food.
- Praise and reward him with the tidbit when he gets there. "That's my boy!" (You can teach a separate command for getting into position on your left side, such as "Close" or "With me." When he is in the position you want (i.e., on your left side), reward him with the tidbit and praise, "That's your Close" or "Good Close!" Eventually the dog will learn to associate "Close"—or whatever command you choose—with being in position on your left side.)
- Show him the tidbit of food. When you have his attention, hold the food ever so slightly above his nose, just high enough that his head is up and he can nibble the food without jumping up. With the food in his face, say his name and give your command for walking on a loose leash (i.e., "Fido, let's go") and then start walking forward.
- Keep your right hand (the one holding the leash) close to your body. This will keep the leash length consistent. As you walk forward, watch the leash. If it begins to tighten, stop walking and stand still. Most likely, your puppy will come to an abrupt halt and look back at you as if to say, "What the heck!"
- Stand still and encourage your puppy back into position with the tidbit of food. Try to avoid moving or turning in circles to reposition your puppy. A dog cannot find your left side (i.e., heel position), if your left side is constantly moving.
- When your puppy is repositioned on your left side, repeat the above-mentioned steps until he is walking beside you without pulling on the leash. When you have taken a few steps, stop, praise, and reward him while he is beside you. If you reward him when he is not in the correct position, you will have inadvertently taught him the wrong association.
- When your puppy is walking beside you, tell him he is smart and clever. Chat sweetly to him to encourage him to walk beside you. Over time, gradually increase the number of steps he is walking on a loose leash, but try not to go so far that he gets out of position

Even growing puppies who are easily distracted can learn to respond to Come quickly and reliably if you keep it extremely rewarding and fun.

and begins pulling on the leash. The goal is to gradually increase the length of time between "Let's go" and rewarding with the treat.

• In the beginning, treats are used to lure the dog into the correct position and show him what you want him to do. Once he understands walking nicely on leash, you can begin keeping the treats in your pocket and rewarding him less often.

PROBLEM BEHAVIORS

In a perfect world, puppies and adult dogs would never get into trouble! In the real world, however, it is unrealistic to expect any dog to go through his entire life without getting into some sort of mischief or developing an annoying habit or two. It is important to remember that dogs, like kids, are first and foremost individuals. No two are alike, and they must be treated as individuals in order to maximize their potential. Their temperaments can fall within a broad range of characteristics, and they can develop their own quirks and idiosyncrasies.

That said, annoying or offensive behaviors do not suddenly appear—they are learned. Dogs do not do anything you do not allow to happen. Puppies and adult dogs do not pee all over the house

just to annoy you. Their brains are not hardwired to be vindictive. If your dog is urinating in the house, it is because he is not housetrained and not effectively supervised.

Equally important, puppies do not *magically* outgrow problems. A puppy who digs holes in your garden will not suddenly stop digging regardless of how much you hope and pray. If you do not want him digging up your favorite rose bushes, you need to modify his environment so he is not put in a position where he is allowed to get himself into trouble.

Excessive Barking

Overall, the Border Collie is by no means a noisy dog. However, it is natural for dogs to bark or otherwise vocalize. They bark for a variety of reasons. They bark when they get excited, when they are playing with other dogs, when the doorbell rings, and to greet you when you arrive home. If you have done enough proper socialization, your Border Collie will not regard every little noise or visitor as a threat.

Your Border Collie's barking will no doubt be reasonable and appropriate, such as to alert you to suspicious intruders or unexpected visitors. Most well-socialized adult Border Collies have an innate ability to protect their territory and will alert bark without being taught to do so. If your Border Collie can be quieted with a single command, you probably do not have much to worry about. Problems arise when your dog is too hyped up to stop barking. Therefore, it is best to curtail any problems immediately. This includes never encouraging your Border Collie

Managing Your Border Collie

The best prevention against future barking problems is smart dog management.

- Never allow your puppy or adult Border Collie to be put in a situation where he is allowed to develop bad habits, such as leaving him in the backyard unsupervised all day where he is inspired to bark at constant stimuli including other dogs barking, a cat on a fence, a bird overhead, leaves falling, neighbors coming and going, and life in general.

- Barking at environmental stimulation is often self-rewarding for the dog. A dog barks at the postman and when the postman leaves the dog thinks, "Look how clever I am! My barking made that man leave!"

- A Border Collie housed indoors can also develop barking habits. If he sits on the furniture and stares out the living room window, he may be encouraged to bark at stimuli, such as neighbors, other dogs going for a walk, kids on bicycles, or the UPS man.

- If your dog barks while in the excitement of play, stop the game immediately. When your dog stops barking, praise, "Good Quiet!" or "Good boy!" Once you have regained control of the situation, begin playing again.

Using something to motivate your dog to stay with you while walking, like a favorite toy or a treat, will positively reward that behavior.

to bark. For instance, when the doorbell rings, avoid asking your Border Collie, "Who's there?" or "Let's go see!" This can excite your Border Collie and encourage him to bark. It may seem like a fun game when he is ten or twelve weeks old, but it is a difficult and annoying behavior to stop once it becomes ingrained.

If your puppy is barking as an attention-seeking behavior, it is best to ignore him until he quiets. Then calmly praise, "Good Quiet!" or "Good boy!" Resist the urge to physically acknowledge your dog's barking by shouting "NO!" or "Quiet!" This will only encourage the unwanted behavior because in a dog's mind negative attention is better than no attention at all. By verbally responding to your dog, you are inadvertently giving the dog what he wants, which is attention.

Avoid soothing or otherwise coddling your Border Collie when he is barking. This too will inadvertently encourage the unwanted behavior. If your dog is barking and you are telling him, "It's okay, honey. Mommy loves you," the dog thinks he is being rewarded for barking. In the dog's mind, he is thinking, "When I bark, my mom tells me it's okay. So I should keep barking." You are inadvertently encouraging the behavior.

Most barking problems can be avoided if you plan ahead and have a clear picture of the behaviors you will and will not accept. However, if your Border Collie has already developed a barking problem and is well on his way to wearing out his welcome, you can try a shaker can as a training aid coupled with positive reinforcement.

Using a Shaker Can

Shaker cans make a lot of noise and that's what you want! The concept is that the noise from the shaker can interrupts your dog's barking, and once the dog's barking behavior is interrupted, you can praise and reward him for not barking.

Shaker cans are easy to make—simply fill an empty soda can with a dozen or so coins or small pebbles and tape the opening closed. As soon as your Border Collie begins to bark—for instance, when the doorbell rings—immediately give a command, such as "Quiet," "Enough," or "No Bark", and shake the can. If done correctly, the noise should be loud enough to startle the dog and interrupt his barking. When he stops barking, immediately praise, "Good Quiet!" or "Good boy!" You can also reinforce the behavior with a tidbit of food, but be sure to do so when the dog is *not* barking. Otherwise, you will be teaching the wrong association and inadvertently reinforcing the barking.

Be sure to keep multiple shaker cans strategically placed around the house—near the telephone, front door, bedroom, living, room, etc.—for convenience and accessibility. Have shaker cans strategically located outdoors, as well.

A word of caution: Be sure to place the shaker cans out of your Border Collie's reach. Aluminum cans are sharp and dangerous when punctured or torn. Border Collies, curious creatures that they are, can cause serious damage to their teeth, tongues, mouths, and

Training Tidbits for Puppies

- Reward only sensible walking. If your puppy is jumping and lunging for the food, hold the food lower and in front of his nose, but do not give it to him until he takes two or three steps without jumping.

- If your puppy is not interested in following you, slow down and be more obvious with the lure. You may need to get a tastier lure or reward more frequently.

- If your puppy freezes on the spot and won't move, do not drag him around or force the issue. Try this: drop the leash and run away while clapping your hands. Very young puppies like to follow their owners. Most likely he will see you running away and try to catch you. When he does, praise him for finding you. "Good boy!" Nonchalantly pick up the leash, start walking and encourage him to walk close to your left side by luring him with a cookie and talking sweetly to him. Take two or three steps, praise, and reward.

stomachs if they chew on the can. Once a Border Collie gets the can open, he may try to swallow the coins, which presents a choking hazard. Most important, never throw the can—or any other objects—at your Border Collie. You may injure or frighten him, and he will most likely learn to fear you.

Chewing

It is hard to imagine an adorable ten-week old Border Collie puppy as a one-dog demolition team. However, do not let their cute looks deceive you. Border Collie puppies, like most puppies, can be incredibly aggressive chewers and wreak havoc in your household. They can destroy drywall, carpet, drapes, and linoleum. They can turn your favorite pillows into confetti, shred your bedspread, destroy electrical cords, and potted plants. They will gladly shred magazines and books and anything else they can get their teeth on—and that is in the 15 minutes it takes you to drive to the post office and back!

If you must leave—even for two minutes—take your Border Collie with you or confine him in a crate, exercise pen, or kennel. Do not put your Border Collie in a position where he can develop bad habits. This point cannot be emphasized enough. Puppies chew, especially when they are teething. If you leave your Border Collie unattended or unconfined while you run to the mailbox or take a quick shower, you should not be surprised when you find the heel missing off your favorite pair of leather shoes.

Prevention is Key

Few owners escape canine ownership without losing a slipper, a pair of rubber galoshes, or a potted plant. Puppies are going to chew. It is a fact of life. However, the key to minimizing destruction and preventing bad habits is management. Never allow your puppy to be put in a position where he can get himself into trouble or develop bad habits. Any puppy left unsupervised is trouble looking for someplace to happen.

If you allow your puppy free run of the house, you should not be surprised when you come home to find epic amounts of destruction. It is equally unfair to scold or otherwise punish a puppy for your temporary lapse of good judgment. Therefore, to foster good habits and minimize destructive behaviors, follow these simply guidelines:
• Before bringing your new puppy home, plan ahead. You should

have an exercise pen or play pen and a crate ready. Do not wait until you decide you need them. If you have a Border Collie, you will need them.

- When you cannot keep a constant watch on your puppy, keep him confined in an exercise pen, play pen, crate, or puppy-proofed area with his favorite chew toy. This includes when you need to jump in the shower for five minutes, while you are making dinner, or when you dash outside for two seconds to move the sprinkler.
- Once your puppy arrives at your home, know where he is and what he is doing at all times. You would never dream of taking your eyes off a toddler, and you should not take your eyes off a Border Collie puppy when he is not safely confined.
- Puppy-proof your home. Puppies are ingenious when it comes to finding items to chew on. Pick up anything and everything your puppy is likely to put in his mouth including shoes, purses, jackets, schoolbooks, candles, rugs, electrical cords, dolls, and so forth.
- Make sure your Border Collie receives plenty of exercise each day. Puppies and adult dogs require daily physical and mental stimulation. Lacking appropriate and adequate exercise, they will release pent up energy through chewing, digging, or barking.

A tip for successful training is to keep training steps small and praise for every tiny step right.

143

Digging

Dogs love to dig. They find it both necessary and pleasurable. Unfortunately, their idea of fun can cause you a significant amount of frustration and heartache, especially when your precious pooch digs his way to China right under your newly planted rose bushes. If you are the type of owner who does not care if your four-legged friend's full-time job is excavating your yard, you have nothing to worry about. Let him dig away, provided, of course, it is safe for him to do so. However, if you prefer not to have potholes in your garden and lawn, prevention is the best solution.

Most often, dogs will dig out of frustration or boredom. Some dig holes to bury their favorite toys or bones. Others will dig in order to find a cool spot to escape the heat. Terriers aren't the only breed that loves to go to ground. Many Border Collies love digging and rooting around in small holes, searching for gophers or moles.

Solutions

Occupy him with something that will stimulate his mind, burn excess energy, and tire him out. Use your imagination to come up with fun games that will stimulate his mind. For instance, purchase a food-dispensing puzzle that allows him to exercise his brain as he tries to outsmart the toy. There are chew toys that can be stuffed with squeeze cheese or peanut butter, and will provide your Border Collie with hours of entertainment. Or, play fun "Find It" games where you hide a tasty tidbit of food under a small box or dish and encourage him to find it. Play hide-and-seek games where you encourage him to find you.

If your Border Collie is digging to find a cool spot to escape the heat, his digging may be the least of your problems. Like many dogs, Border Collies do not tolerate hot weather. You need to get him out of the heat and provide him with a cool spot, such as an air-conditioned room or a cool grassy area with plenty of shade.

Many dogs are attracted to the smell of chicken and steer manure and love to dig and roll in fresh soil and newly fertilized gardens. The best solution for digging in gardens and flower boxes is prevention. Do not allow your Border Collie free access to the garden areas where he can dig and wreak havoc. An alternative is to install a small fence around the garden, or fence off a section of yard just for him where he can dig and dig until his heart's content.

Jumping Up

Puppies and adult dogs love to jump on people. It's their way of getting close to your face and saying "Hi!" with a wet tongue. Licking faces is a natural behavior for dogs when they greet each other, and they don't understand that humans frequently take offense. Of course, if you don't mind your dog jumping on you—and some owners don't—then you have nothing to worry about. However, what you think is cute, harmless puppy behavior is far from amusing if your Border Collie weighs 50 pounds and has four muddy feet. An adult dog outweighs most kids and more than a few adults. For this reason alone, you should discourage your dog from jumping.

The key is to discourage all occasions of jumping up. If you do

Border Collies are not known to be noisy dogs, but a barking problem may still develop for any number of reasons. Identify them, and you can train away the problem.

not want your adult dog to jump on you, do not allow the behavior when he is puppy. It is equally unfair to allow him to jump on you, but correct him for jumping on visitors. Or to allow him to jump on you today but not tomorrow when you are wearing white pants.

The Importance of Chew Toys

There are a variety of chew toys available in all sizes and shapes that will entertain your Border Collie for an hour or two. Chew toys will satisfy your puppy's need to gnaw on something while diverting him from chewing on inappropriate items. While some chew toys are better than others, there is no scientific formula for finding the right chew toy. Most times it is a matter of trial and error. Avoid toys or bones that are too hard and may crack your dog's teeth, or ones that are too small or break apart and present choking hazards.

• Commercial chew products come in a wide variety of shapes, sizes, and types, including beef muscle, pig ears, smoked hog hide, dehydrated pig snouts, and tightly rolled rawhide. Some colored rawhide chews can stain carpets and furnishings. Choking or intestinal blockage with rawhide chews is rare, but not impossible. Therefore, always monitor your dog when chewing rawhide (or any chewy). When rawhide becomes soft, replace it with another chewy. Allow the soft, soggy piece to dry and harden before reusing it.

• Cow hooves, while a popular canine favorite, are hard and can chip or break your dog's teeth.

• Specially designed rigid nylon and rubber bones and toys are excellent for satisfying your puppy's need to chew.

• Rope toys and tugs are often made of 100-percent cotton. They are frequently flavored to make them more attractive to your puppy or adult dog. Some have plaque-fighting fluoride floss woven into the rope to deep clean your dog's teeth and gums. Be careful your puppy cannot shred the cotton ropes, which may be a potential choking hazard.

• Plush toys vary in their durability. Some are easily shredded by tenacious, seek-and-destroy Border Collies who can chew out the squeaky part in record time. If your puppy is likely to shred, disembowel, and attempt to consume plush toy innards, opt for the durable models when choosing these toys.

• A super-size carrot is often a good chew toy for young puppies. They are tasty, durable, easily digestible, and puppies seem to love them. Stay away from raisins and grapes, which can be toxic in certain quantities.

As soon as you see your puppy coming to greet you, crouch down and make a fuss of him. As you do this, slip your thumb in his collar under his chin (your thumb should be pointing down toward the ground) and apply gentle pressure so he cannot jump up. Give him praise only when all four feet are on the ground. Your praise should be sincere, but not overly enthusiastic. Otherwise, you are likely to wind him up even more.

To prevent your puppy (or adult dog) from jumping on visitors, make sure he is on leash before you open the door. This allows you to control his behavior without grabbing at his collar. When he sits nicely without pawing or mauling your guests, calmly raise and reward him with a tasty tidbit. "That's my good boy!" You can incorporate the entire family by allowing them to practice being a visitor. One at a time, have them go outside, ring the doorbell, then you open the door and invite them in as if they were a visitor. Besides making it a fun family venture, you will eventually have a puppy that grows into an adult dog that does not grope your guests.

Small children like to run, flail their arms, and make loud squealing noises. This type of behavior is especially attractive to young puppies. Most likely, a young child will not be able to control a jumping puppy, let alone a 50-pound dog. Therefore, always supervise children and manage your dog so he is not put in a position where he can develop bad habits.

Puppies and adult dogs love to jump

up when you arrive home. To curtail some jumping, stash a small container filled with dry dog food outside near the door. Before going inside, grab a handful of food. When you open the door, toss the food on the floor inside the entry. Your puppy or adult dog will run for the treats. You slip inside without being mauled, giving yourself a few seconds to gather your senses, drop your purse or groceries, and prepare for an onslaught of kisses.

Running Off or Not Coming When Called

Border Collies who run away from their owners or refuse to come when called can create an enormous amount of frustration and angst for their owners. The good news is that it is one of the easiest problems to solve. The key is to never allow your puppy to be put in a situation where he can develop the bad habit of running off. Each and every time you go outside, your puppy should be on leash. If

Establishing a safe chew toy habit in puppyhood will prevent a lot of unwanted and unnecessary chewing throughout your Border Collie's life.

you want your puppy to run around and explore his surroundings—he should be dragging his leash or a lightweight long-line. If your puppy starts to wander off, simply step on the long-line and reel him back in.

Teach Your Puppy Right From Wrong

If you allow your Border Collie puppy supervised excursions into the rest of the house, you will be able to monitor his whereabouts and, in the process, provide him with appropriate chew toys. If, for instance, you are watching television, have one or two chew toys available for your puppy. You may need to encourage him by showing him the toy. When you see him settle down to chew on it, calmly praise him. Then allow him to chew without interruption. You can try tethering him to the leg of the couch or coffee table with a lightweight leash to prevent him from wandering off.

Until your puppy is reliable, it is wise not to give him free run of the house. Remember, puppies are individuals. It is impossible to arbitrarily put an age on when a puppy is reliably trained. Some puppies have a stronger desire to chew than others. A general guideline is about one year of age. However, much of this will also depend on how conscientious and committed you are to managing your puppy's environment, instilling good behaviors, and discouraging unwanted behaviors.

As your puppy grows and matures, his desire to chew will diminish. It is important, however, to continue giving him bones and chew toys throughout his life to exercise his jaws, keep his teeth clean, and entertain him for a few hours.

If your adult dog has already developed the annoying habit of running off or ignoring your come command, a leash or long-line will prevent him from continuing to do so. You will then need to go back and re-teach him to come when called. You should also never get in the habit of chasing your puppy, or allowing your kids to chase your puppy. Dogs think this is a fun game, but it teaches a dog to run away from you, which is not only annoying but also dangerous. A puppy or adult dog that runs away from his owner can easily dart into traffic, causing serious injury to himself.

SEEKING PROFESSIONAL HELP

Despite your best efforts to raise a well-behaved Border Collie, there will undoubtedly be times when things go terribly wrong, and you may need to call in an expert. Some problems, such as aggression and separation anxiety are difficult and complicated areas of canine behavior that require expert guidance. These behaviors are multi-faceted and often have overlapping causes. For instance, genetics, lack of socialization, sexual maturity/frustration, lack of obedience training, inappropriate corrections, and pain are a few of the reasons why dogs might display aggression. Dogs with true separation anxiety issues can work themselves into a frenzy. They become anxious, salivate, pace, whine, bark, and work themselves into an uncontrollable state of panic, destroying anything and everything they can get their teeth and paws on including couches, walls, doors, rugs, and plants.

If you feel you and your dog need expert advice, don't hesitate to seek it. There is no shame in asking guidance from someone who makes their bread and butter training dogs. You and your dog will be much happier in the long run.

This Border Collie thoroughly enjoys a game of tug with a safe and durable hard nylon chew toy.

Understanding Who Is Who

To find the right dog expert, one must first sort through the terminology. Armed with the proper information, you can make an informed and educated decision as to which professional is best qualified to help you meet your training goals.

• Professional **dog trainers** and **dog obedience instructors** are often lumped into the same category. There is a fine line of distinction. However, for the sake of discussion, they both train dogs. They are hands on. They teach basic obedience commands, recondition and retrain behaviors, offer solutions to common problems including aggression, separation anxiety, not coming when called, chewing, digging, jumping up, nipping, and so on. They may teach group obedience classes and/or offer private lessons. Most of them have dogs, and many are involved in the sport of dogs. Many dog obedience instructors focus on puppy training, basic pet obedience, and competitive dog sports, such as obedience, herding, field work, tracking, and so on. They may or may not be members of an organization, such as the National Association of Dog Obedience Instructors. Most trainers learn techniques from other trainers, apprenticeships, academic studies, or a combination.

• **Applied animal behaviorists** take scientific knowledge about animal behavior and apply it to real life issues, such as digging, chewing, barking, jumping, aggression, separation anxiety, and house soiling. They also have post-graduate degrees in animal behavior, such as biology or zoology. Their study is not limited to dogs, and many teach at universities and work in zoos, animal shelters, and research facilities. They may or may not own a dog, and they may or may not have ever obedience-trained a dog.

Puppies and dogs jump up on people to express and solicit affection. This is a problem that is easily solved.

151

As sweet as your dog may be, if his manners are extremely poor, it's time to consult a professional. You'll be glad you did – and so will your dog.

Many animal behaviorists consult owners over the telephone for a fee. They generally work one-on-one with the owner, as opposed to group classes.

- **Animal behavior consultants** are similar to applied animal behaviorists but without the post-graduate academic degree. They use scientific knowledge about animal behavior to evaluate, manage, and modify a wide variety of canine behaviors including aggression, separation anxiety, jumping, nipping, and house training problems. Many work with other animals including cats, horses, and birds. They may or may not own a dog, and they may or may not have ever obedience-trained a dog. Many are certified by organizations such as the International Association of Animal Behavior Consultants (IAABC).

- **Veterinary Behaviorists** are veterinarians who have successfully completed the requirements for board certification in the American

Veterinary Medical Association (AVMA) specialty of animal behavior. Veterinary behaviorists are medical experts with a special interest in animal behavior. They work with a number of different animals, including dogs. The American College of Veterinary Behaviorists (ACVB) is the official certifying organization for veterinary behaviorists.

Finding a Behaviorist or Consultant

- Contact professional organizations for a referral, such as the American College of Veterinary Behaviorists, American Veterinary Medical Association, Animal Behavior Society, International Association of Animal Behavior Consultants, or the Association of Pet Behaviour Counsellors (United Kingdom).

- Many universities and colleges have applied animal behaviorists on staff. Contact them for referrals.

- Many behaviorists and consultants work with veterinarians. Ask your vet for a referral.

ADVANCED TRAINING AND ACTIVITIES
With Your Border Collie

order Collies are intelligent, energetic, and love to work. An excellent desire to please coupled with a strong human/canine bond, high energy, and a strong work ethic allows them to succeed in a variety of canine sports. That makes finding the perfect sport or pastime for you and your Border Collie relatively easy. After all, there are countless canine activities from which to choose. The physical, mental, and financial demands of canine activities vary dramatically, and how much you are willing to invest is always a personal choice. It may take a few tries at different activities, but chances are there is a canine sport—or two!—with your Border Collie's name on it. National clubs and registries, such as the American Kennel Club, Kennel Club in the U.K., and the American Border Collie Association, offer a wide variety of all breed and breed-specific canine sports and competitions in which your Border Collie can compete.

ORGANIZED COMPETITIONS

Training and competing with your Border Collie allows you to enhance the human / canine relationship, build a strong and mutually respectful relationship, and have a great deal of fun in the process. You might even ignite the competitive spark and find yourself hooked on canine competitions. There are plenty of canine sports you can enter that will showcase your dog's agility, athleticism, and intelligence. Through American Kennel Club-sanctioned events alone, you and your Border Collie can participate in agility, Canine Good Citizen, conformation, herding, obedience, rally obedience, and tracking.

Agility

Agility is one of the fastest growing sports for dogs, and one of the most exciting, fast-paced canine sports for spectators. It is an extension of obedience but without all the formality and precision. Agility courses are more reminiscent of equestrian

The History of Agility

The origin of Agility can be traced across the Atlantic to Great Britain. The sport originated in 1978 as a small-scale demonstration in the main ring at the prestigious Crufts Dog Show. The show committee wanted an entertainment venue to fill the spare time between the Obedience championships and the Group judging. As a result, John Varley, a member of the Crufts dog show committee and an experienced showman, and Peter Meanwell, an experienced working trial competitor, designed a challenging obstacle course, borrowing many elements from equestrian events. The challenging obstacles and fast-paced dogs hooked spectators and the rest, as they say, is history

courses that include assorted jumps and hurdles. In agility, dogs demonstrate their agile nature and versatility by maneuvering through a timed obstacle course of jumps, tunnels, A-frames, weave poles, teeter-totters, ramps, and a pause box. Unlike obedience, agility handlers are permitted to talk to their dogs, and even give multiple commands.

Like a navigator, a good agility handler aims the dog toward each successive obstacle while trying to regulate the dog's precision, and, of course, staying the heck out of the way of a fast moving Border Collie. A perfect score in any class is 100, and competitors are faulted if they go over the allotted course time or receive a penalty, such as taking an obstacle out of sequence, missing a contact zone, touching the dog, and so forth.

All-breed agility trials are the most common type of trial and are open to all AKC breeds and varieties of dogs. Specialty trials are restricted to dogs of a specific breed or varieties of one breed. There are two types of classes offered at an agility trial: Standard and Jumpers with Weaves. The Standard class has a pause box and contact obstacles—those yellow contact zones at each end of the obstacle. The dog must place at least one paw in the contact zone—otherwise, he receives a fault. The goal is to encourage safety in training and in running the course. The Jumpers with Weaves class also has a variety of obstacles but does not have contact obstacles or a pause box that slow the competitor's forward momentum. Within each agility class there are different levels of competition:

- **Novice.** For the dog who is just starting in agility. There are 13 to 15 obstacles on the course, and the focus is on completing each obstacle with a minimum of handling skill required.
- **Open**. For the dog who has completed the Novice level. There are 16 to 18 obstacles on the course, and the degree of difficulty increases. The Open class also requires significantly more handling skills than the Novice class.
- **Excellent.** For the dog who has completed the Open level. There are 18 to 20 obstacles, the degree of difficulty increases significantly, and the focus is to provide competitors with the opportunity to demonstrate their superior training, communication, and handling skills.

For the die-hard agility competitor, the **Master Agility Champion** title (MACH) is the pinnacle of agility competition. To achieve a MACH title, a dog must exhibit speed and consistency on the agility course. They must receive a minimum of 750 champion points and 20 double-qualifying scores from the Excellent B Standard and Excellent B Jumpers and Weaves class. To put it in layman's terms, handlers receive one champion point for each full second under the standard course time. They can double the championship points received if they place first in their class. Die-hard competitors can continue to earn MACH titles that indicate the number of times a dog has met the requirements of the MACH title. For instance, a dog who earns 1500 champion points and 40 double-qualifying scores would earn a MACH 2.

Colorful jumps are just part of a varied agility course that dogs and handlers thrill to compete over.

The best way to get started in agility is to join a local dog-training club or visit an agility training facility.

Canine Good Citizen

If you enjoy training your Border Collie, but organized competitions are not your cup of tea, the American Kennel Club's Canine Good Citizen® (CGC) Program might be a viable alternative. Implemented in 1989, the CGC Program is a public education and certification program designed to demonstrate that the companion dog can be a respected member of the community. The CGC Program encourages owners to develop a positive and worthwhile relationship with their dogs by rewarding responsible dog ownership and good pet manners. It is designed to encourage owners to get involved with and obedience train their dogs.

While the program does not involve the formality or precision of competitive obedience, it does lay the foundation for good pet manners and is often used as a stepping stone for other canine activities, such as obedience, rally obedience, and agility. Owners can imporove the human/canine relationship by training and readying their dog for this relatively simple test.

The CGC program is designed to encourage owners to get involved with and train their dogs to have good manners. It is a noncompetitive, 10-part test that evaluates your Border Collie's behavior in practical situations at home, in public, and in the presence of unfamiliar people and other dogs. The pass/fail test is designed to assess a Border Collie's reaction to distractions, friendly strangers, and supervised isolation. Additionally, a Border Collie must sit politely while being petted, walk on a loose leash, walk through a crowd, and respond to basic obedience commands including sit, down, stay, and come. The evaluator also inspects the dog to determine if he is clean and groomed. Both purebred and mixed-breed dogs are eligible to participate. While there is no age limit, dogs must be old enough to have received their immunizations.

Herding

Sheepdog trials have come a long way since the first trial was held at Bala in North Wales more than 130 years ago. However, their primary function remains the same—to provide a competitive venue to determine the working ability and skill of herding dogs and their handlers. Simply put, a herding trial is a chance to prove that your dog is better than the competition. Ultimately, sheepdog trials help to establish a guide for better breeding and training by encouraging a high standard of performance in herding dogs, and by allowing owners to study the better dogs and evaluate the qualities most desired.

Trials are designed to parallel the everyday work of a sheepdog on a hill farm—the type of working environment you are likely to see in the border lands between England and Scotland. Every aspect of the trial is derived from farm work,

Sheepdog trials are held across the country so owners can watch their Border Collies' true colors shine through.

and while each trial is a bit different, they normally consist of an outrun, lift, fetch, drive, pen, and shed.

The International Sheep Dog Society (ISDS) puts on four national trials annually in England, Ireland, Scotland, and Wales. The top competitors from each national trial form the four teams that compete in the International Sheep Dog Trials—currently the world's premier sheepdog trialing event.

In the United States, sheepdog trials are fashioned after the British trials. The United States Border Collie Handler's Association (USBCHA) trials are considered to be the true test of working Border Collies. The National Finals, sponsored by the USBCHA, is run annually to select America's champion herding dogs.

AKC Herding Tests

As Border Collies become increasingly popular as pets, many owners are dabbling in AKC-sponsored events designed to test a Border Collie's herding instinct. While these tests and trials are artificial simulations of working pastoral or farm conditions, they are not really reflective of true farm work. However, they do provide a standardized test by which owners can measure their dog's inherent herding abilities and training.

The AKC herding program has two major divisions: Herding Tests and Herding Trials.

- Herding Tests are non-competitive tests that are intended for dogs with little or no prior herding experience. Dogs must, however, show a sustained interest in herding livestock. Within this division, owners can earn two certifications: HT (Herding Tested Dog), which indicates a dog has shown herding instinct and is under basic control, and a PT (Pretrial Tested Dog), which indicates that a dog and handler worked together as a team, and the dog had a modest amount of training but not enough to compete in the lowest level trial.

- Herding Trials are competitive trials intended for dogs with substantial training. Dogs must demonstrate the ability to move and control livestock. The titles awarded in each division are: HS (Herding Started), HI (Herding Intermediate), HX (Herding Excellent), and H CH (Champion). For an H CH, a dog must have earned an HX and at least 15 championship points in the advanced classes.

OBEDIENCE

Every aspect of dog ownership involves some form of obedience training, yet the obedience ring seldom receives the public awareness and media attention of other canine events. An obedience

Herding Tidbits

- The first recorded sheepdog trial took place at Bala in North Wales in October 1873.

- Ten dogs competed, and three hundred spectators turned out to watch Mr. James Thomson, a Scotsman, and his dog, Tweed, win the earliest recorded dog trial.

- The first Scottish trial was held in the early 1870s

- The first English trial was held in 1876

- In 1906, the International Sheep Dog Society (ISDS) was founded.

- Sheepdog trials were first introduced to the United States in September 1880 in Philadelphia, PA

- The first "official" sheepdog trial was held in Bennington, Vt., in 1928, and 1,500 people gathered to watch 7 dogs compete.

competition goes well beyond the CGC Program and tests a Border Collie's ability to perform a prescribed set of exercises in a formal environment. One might compare it to the formal and elegant equine dressage tests with owners achieving a harmonious relationship with their animals, all the while observing meticulous attention to minute details.

In addition to enriching the bond and relationship between a dog and handler, obedience training is designed to emphasize "the usefulness of purebred dogs as the ultimate companion and helpmate to man, and as a means of recognizing that dogs have been trained to behave in the home, in public places, and in the presence of other dogs," according to the American Kennel Club. There are three levels of competitive obedience:

- **The Novice Level:** The dog is required to heel on and off leash at a normal, fast, and slow pace; come when called; stand for a physical examination by the judge; and do a sit-stay and a down-stay with other dogs. Other than giving commands, handlers are not allowed to talk to their dog during the exercise, nor are they allowed to use toys, treats, or other training aids in the ring. Dogs who complete this level receive a Companion Dog (CD) title.

- **The Open Level:** The Open class is quite a bit more difficult than the Novice class because all exercises are performed off leash. A dog will be required to do similar heelwork exercises as in the Novice class, as well as a retrieve exercise, a drop on recall, a high jump, broad jump, and a sit-stay and a down-stay with other dogs while the handlers are out of sight. Dogs who complete this level receive a Companion Dog Excellent (CDX) title.

Border Collies and their owners frequent organized herding tests and trials – and come home with many awards.

- **The Utility Level:** Utility is the final and most difficult and challenging level of training. The exercises include scent discrimination, directed jumping, retrieving, hand signals, and a moving stand and examination. Completing this level awards your dog a Utility Dog (UD) title.

If you've gotten this far, you are seriously committed to the sport of obedience, and you may decide to work toward a Utility Dog Excellent (UDX) or Obedience Trial Championship title (OTCH)—the crème de la crème of obedience competition. While it is considered the most prestigious title, it has also proven to be the most elusive crown since its inception in 1977.

The best way to get involved in obedience is to sign up for a dog obedience class or join a local dog obedience club. If you are interested in the sport of competitive obedience, it is helpful to find a trainer that competes in the sport and teaches competitive obedience classes.

Rally Obedience

Rally obedience is the newest AKC event. It is a combination of agility and obedience, though emphasis is less on speed and precision and more on how well dogs and handlers perform together as a team. It was created with the average dog owner in mind, to help promote a positive human/canine relationship with an emphasis on fun and excitement. It also takes the pressure off of competing, while still allowing owners to showcase their Border Collies' obedience skills.

Performing off-lead is required in obedience competitions.

In rally obedience, the dog and handler move through a course that has been designed by the rally judge. They proceed at their own pace through a course of designated stations—between 10 and 20, depending on the level. A sign at each of these stations provides instructions on the skill that is to be performed, such as "Halt and Sit," "Halt," "Sit," "Down," "Right Turn," "About Right Turn," or "Perform a 270-degree left turn while heeling."

Unlike traditional obedience competitions, handlers are permitted to talk to their dogs, use praise, clap their hands, pat their own legs, or use any verbal means of communication and body language throughout the performance. Handlers may not touch their dogs or make physical corrections. Any dog who is eligible for AKC registration can enter rally obedience.

Showing (Conformation)

Conformation shows (dog shows) are the signature events of the competitive dog world. The conformation ring, commonly referred to as the breed ring, provides a forum for breeders and handlers to showcase the best in breeding stock. These animals are evaluated as potential breeding stock and are usually incorporated into future breeding programs in an effort to improve the breed. For this reason, dogs competing in conformation may not be spayed or neutered.

How Dog Shows Work

The best way to understand the conformation ring is to think of it in terms of an elimination process. Each Border Collie enters a regular class and is evaluated against the Border Collie breed standard. For the newcomer, it often appears as if the dogs are competing against one another. And, in a sense they are. However, the judge is not comparing the quality of one Border Collie against the quality of another. The judge is evaluating each Border Collie against the breed standard and how closely each dog measures up to the ideal Border Collie as outlined in that standard.

The regular classes are divided by sex, with males and females judged separately. The male dogs are always judged first and, after being examined by the judge, are placed first through fourth according to how well they measure up to the breed standard in the judge's opinion. After the males have been judged, the females go through the same process.

After the regular classes have been judged, the first place winners of each class are brought back to the ring to compete against one another in the Winners Class. The dog selected is the Winners Dog and is awarded championship points. A Reserve Winners Dog is also chosen but does not receive points unless the Winners Dog, for any reason, is disallowed or disqualified. The same process is then repeated with the female dogs, resulting in a Winners Bitch and Reserve Winners Bitch.

The Winners Dog and Winners Bitch go back into the ring with any champions entered to compete for the Best of

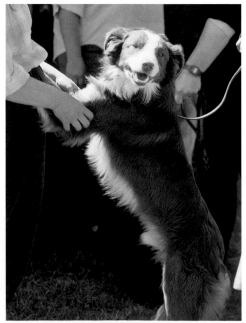

Dog shows are competitive events where dogs and handlers must look and act their best, but there are still moments of relaxation, even in the ring.

Breed award. If either the Winners Dog or Winners Bitch wins Best of Breed or Best of Winners, they may also win more points. The Best of Breed dog or bitch then goes on to the Group. The Group winners are then judged with Group placements—first through fourth—being awarded in each of the seven groups. The first place Group winners compete for the most coveted and most prestigious award: Best in Show.

Earning a Championship

To attain an AKC Championship title, a Border Collie must win a total of 15 points. Only the Winners Dog and Winners Bitch receive points. The number of points earned at each show is predetermined by a point schedule that varies from region to region.

The number of points awarded at each show depends on the breed, the number of dogs entered in the competition, and the location of the show. For example, points awarded to a Border Collie in New York will differ from the number of points awarded in California. The number of points that can be won at a show is between one and five. Three-, four-, and five-point wins are considered *majors*. One- and two-point wins are considered *minors*. Of the 15 points required for a Championship title, six or more of the points must be majors. The remaining points may be attained in any combination, including major or minor wins, but must be won under different judges than the two major wins. Therefore, you need to win points under at least three different judges. A Border Collie can add to the number of points won in the Winners Class if he also wins Best of Breed, Best of Opposite Sex, or Best of Winners. Once the requirements are met and officially confirmed, then a championship certificate is issued for the individual dog.

Tracking

The first AKC licensed tracking test took place on June 13, 1936. Today, tracking is a popular sport that tests a Border Collie's ability to recognize and track a human scent over varying terrains and climatic changes. It is designed to showcase a dog's intelligence and extremely high level of scent capability. The goal is for the dog to follow a scented track and locate an article left at the end of the trail by a tracklayer.

Border Collies can earn three different tracking titles: Tracking Dog (TD), Tracking Dog Excellent (TDX), and Variable Surface Tracking

Three Types of AKC Confirmation Shows

- All-breed shows are exactly what the name implies. They are open to over 150 breeds and varieties of dogs recognized by the American Kennel Club, and include shows such as the prestigious Westminster Kennel Club. These are the types of conformation shows you are most likely to see on television.

- Specialty shows are for one specific breed, such as the Border Collie. Most often, local, regional, or national breed-specific clubs sponsor these shows.

- Group shows: shows that are limited to dogs belonging to one of the seven groups. For example, a working group show would feature only breeds belonging to the working group.

Crufts

Billed as the "Greatest Dog Show in the World," the Crufts dog show is officially recognized by the Guinness Book of Records as the largest one too, with more than 24,000 dogs entered. The four-day event covers 20 acres with nearly 400 vendor booths and attracts more than 120,000 visitors.

(VST). If a Border Collie successfully completes all three tracking titles, he earns the prestigious title of Champion Tracker (CT).

To earn a TD title, a Border Collie must follow a track laid by a human tracklayer. The track must be 440 to 500 yards with three to five changes of direction, and the track must be *aged*—the time between when a track is laid and the dog can begin scenting—at least 30 minutes but not more than two hours.

A TDX title is the next level and slightly more difficult than a TD. It is earned when a Border Collie follows a track that is between 800 and 1,000 yards and between three and five hours old. The TDX track must have five to seven directional changes and also includes the additional challenge of human cross tracks which, as the name implies, is a human track that crosses the primary track. A dog must also locate four articles rather than the one article required for a TD.

TD and TDX tracks are laid through open fields and wilderness areas and include varying terrain conditions, such as gullies, plowed land, woods, and vegetation. However, urban sprawl has severely limited those spaces in some parts of the country. As a result, the Variable Surface Tracking (VST) title was designed to utilize industrial and office parks, college campuses, and so forth. To earn a VST title, dogs who have already earned a TD title must follow a track that is 600 to 800 yards in length and between three to five hours old. The track may take them down a street, between

Tracking challenges a dog's intelligence and scenting ability as he follows an aged, scented track over changing terrain.

buildings, across a college campus, asphalt parking lot, concrete sidewalk, and the like.

Unlike obedience and agility titles that require a dog and handler to qualify three times, a Border Collie only needs to complete one track successfully to earn each title. If you and your Border Collie love the great outdoors, tracking might be the sport for you. The best way to get involved in tracking is to contact a local dog obedience club or a national organization, such as the American Border Collie Club, American Kennel Club, The Kennel Club, or Canadian Kennel Club.

OTHER FUN SPORTS FOR YOU AND YOUR BORDER COLLIE

If you've considered all the AKC events and you're still looking for more fun sports, try some these fun events. One is sure to pique the interest of you and your Border Collie.

Canine Freestyle

Just when you think no one could possibly come up with yet another canine sport, along comes another one! Canine Freestyle is an exciting and invigorating team sport that allows you and your Border Collie to kick up your heels, so to speak. In the simplest terms, Canine Freestyle is a choreographed performance between a dog and handler that is set to music.

Don't let the catchy name fool you. Canine Freestyle is more than dogs heeling to music. The sport is patterned after Olympic skating with dogs and handlers performing twists, turns, leg kicks, pivots, and other cool and creative maneuvers. These maneuvers are entwined with basic obedience commands, such as heelwork, sits, downs, and fronts. Many advanced competitors teach their dogs to crawl, back up, wave, bow, side step, bounce, rollover, spin, and play dead. Freestyle routines are varied and creatively choreographed with an emphasis on the special and unique bond that exists between a dog and handler. The fun is limited only to your imagination and creativity!

As with other canine sports, Canine Freestyle offers a number of divisions and categories to suit a dog and handler's varying levels of experience. Several organizations promote Canine Freestyle, with styles varying between the organizations. For additional information, contact the Canine Freestyle Federation, Inc. (CFF) or the World Canine Freestyle Organization, Inc. (WCFO).

Flyball

Invented in the late 1970s, Flyball is yet another exhilarating choice in the list of entertaining sports you can do with your Border Collie. It is the sport for all tennis ball-loving dogs! To say Flyball is fast-paced is an understatement. It is a high-octane relay race that showcases a Border Collie's speed and agility. Don't worry—your Border Collie does all of the running in this sport! It is a team sport rather than an individual competition, and an equally thrilling and entertaining spectator sport.

The course consists of four hurdles (small jumps) spaced approximately 10 feet apart. Fifteen feet beyond the last hurdle is a spring-loaded box that contains a tennis ball. Just as in any relay race, the fastest team to successfully complete the game wins. The goal is for each dog to take a turn running the relay by leaping each of the four hurdles and then hitting a pedal or lever with his paw to trigger the box, which shoots a tennis ball up in the air. Once the dog catches the ball in his mouth, he races back over the four hurdles to the finish line, where the next dog is anxiously awaiting his turn.

The first team to have all four dogs run without errors wins the heat. If a dog misses a hurdle or fails to retrieve the ball, he must repeat his turn. For additional information contact the North American Flyball Association or the British Flyball Association.

Skijoring

In its simplest terms, skijoring is being pulled on skis by one or more dogs in harness. The great thing about skijoring is almost any dog (over 30 pounds) can participate, which makes it ideal for the athletic Border Collie. With a minimum amount of equipment, an eager Border Collie, and a pair of cross- country skis, you can have the time of your life—while increasing the human / canine bond.

Skijoring is fairly easy to learn, but it does require some basic skills. You will need to be somewhat proficient on cross-country skis, your Border Collie will need to be accustomed to wearing a harness, and he will need to know how to pull. It is helpful if your dog has some basic obedience skills, as well. It's fun, it's exhilarating, and it's the perfect canine sport if you and your Border Collie enjoy the great outdoors.

Canine freestyle is a kind of dancing with dogs, where routines are shaped through play and training.

Swimming

Swimming is an excellent activity for cooling off, burning calories, and sharing quality time with your Border Collie. Be forewarned, not all Border Collies will take to the water like, well, a fish. You may need to take it slowly and introduce your Border Collie to water playfully and gradually. It is never advisable to toss your young Border Collie in the water. It is highly likely that doing so will frighten him—not to mention the possibility of injuring him and turning him off to swimming and water activities for the rest of his life.

For the reluctant Border Collie, try to find a swimming pool, lake, or shallow pond that has a gentle sloping bank. Kiddy pools or wading pools are also excellent for the hesitant swimmer. Try to encourage your Border Collie to wade in with you or throw a floatable toy for him to retrieve, being careful in the beginning to toss it close to the bank of the pond or edge of the pool. If you toss it too far, it is likely he will find the task of retrieving too daunting.

Border Collies love the tempo and athleticism of Frisbee in the back yard or at a competition.

The ocean is wonderful for invigorating walks on the beach and dips in the water. Your Border Collie may be content to dip his feet in the foam. Or he may be more adventurous and take a full body plunge. It is important to keep your Border Collie close to shore regardless of his superior athleticism and swimming capabilities. Riptides and undercurrents are unpredictable, and your Border Collie can quickly wade into trouble.

Most dogs will play until they exhaust themselves and collapse into a heap of sleep. Therefore, it is important to watch for signs that your dog is getting tired, such as slowing down or frantically slapping the water with his front feet. A lifejacket designed specifically for dogs may give you some peace of mind while providing a safety net for your water-loving companion.

Walking, Jogging, Hiking

Border Collies have enormous amounts of energy and a strong work ethic. As a result, they make ideal exercise companions, and no doubt, both you and your Border Collie will benefit from the exercise and companionship. It is worth reiterating that Border Collies can and do suffer from heat-induced illnesses. Therefore, if you plan to include your Border Collie in your daily walks or jogs, it is advisable to limit these activities to cooler parts of the day, such as the early morning or evening. Equally important, hot sidewalks and roads can burn a Border Collie's feet, causing an enormous amount of pain and discomfort. If the sidewalks and roadways are too hot for your bare feet, chances are they will be too hot for your Border Collie's feet. How far a Border Collie can walk, jog, or hike will depend on his age, physical condition, the terrain covered, and the weather. An extended hike through rough terrain and rocky surfaces may be a piece of cake for the conditioned dogs, but too taxing for some canine couch potatoes. It is always a good idea to carry plenty of fluid for both you and your Border Collie.

CANINE CAREERS

Herding is a Border Collie's ancestry, but the breed has been known to excel in assistance and therapy work, as well.

Assistance Dogs (AKA Service Dogs)

The terms *therapy dogs* and *service dogs* are often used interchangeably, but there is a significant difference. The Americans with Disabilities Act uses the term *service dog* to define a dog who has been "individually trained to work or perform tasks for the benefit of a person with a disability." Professionals within the industry often refer to them as *assistance dogs*. Therapy dogs provide companionship and emotional support, but do not perform tasks and federal law does not legally define them.

Under the umbrella of assistance dogs there are four categories: therapy dogs, guide dogs, service dogs, and hearing dogs. While you occasionally see Border Collies performing some of these tasks, the last three categories usually employ Golden Retrievers, Labrador Retrievers, or German Shepherds. If your Border Collie has the right temperament,

Some Border Collies don't like water, but for those that do, swimming is another opportunity to play and have fun.

you might want to explore the area of therapy work.

Therapy Dogs

Therapy is an important area in which Border Collies can help enhance the human/canine bond by providing unconditional love, companionship, and emotional support to nursing home, hospital, assisted living, and mental health residents. Owners volunteering with their Border Collies make regularly scheduled visits and brighten the lives of residents by providing stimulation, companionship, and a vehicle for conversation and interaction.

How could a face like this not make someone feel better? Border Collies can make excellent therapy dogs.

Only Border Collies who are well-mannered and have a sound temperament should undertake this work. While it is personally satisfying to see how dogs can brighten the lives of residents, 90 percent of the work is done by the dogs, and they must have the physical and mental fortitude to cope with strange noises and smells, distractions, and oftentimes erratic behaviors. Additionally, dogs must be willing to accept a considerable amount of attention, petting, and touching from strangers. It helps if your Border Collie has a foundation of basic obedience training or his Canine Good Citizen certificate. While the AKC does offer Canine Good Citizen certifications, they do not certify therapy dogs. There are independent organizations that certify therapy dogs. National organizations, including Therapy Dogs Incorporated, Therapy Dogs International, and the Delta Society, can provide additional information on certifications and requirements.

Dog Sports and Safety

Before beginning any physically challenging activity with your Border Collie, it is prudent to take him to the veterinarian for a thorough examination. Joint problems, such as hip and elbow dysplasia are problematic in some Border Collies and should be of paramount importance and concern for owners. They may preclude your Border Collie from some of the more physically demanding activities. Low-stress activities are wonderful for puppies, but young dogs (generally under the age of two) should not be allowed to jump. Too much pressure on developing joints and limbs can injure your puppy and lead to lifelong problems.

HEALTH

of Your Border Collie

Like good-quality nutrition, there is no substitute for regular veterinary care. There are any number of infectious diseases, parasites, and serious ailments that can impair your Border Collie's health, but today's veterinarians have the academic training and expertise necessary to reduce and prevent serious illnesses, helping to keep your Border Collie in the best health possible.

CHOOSING A VETERINARIAN

It is never too early to begin looking for a veterinarian. If your new Border Collie has yet to arrive at your home or you have recently moved—you will want to find a veterinarian before you actually need one. It is never a good idea to be scanning the yellow pages when your Border Collie is sick or injured. Just as you spent a great deal of time and energy finding the right Border Collie breeder, you will need to invest time and energy finding a suitable veterinarian with whom you and your precious pooch will feel comfortable and can build a mutually trusting and respectful relationship. Think about what you want in a veterinarian. Perhaps proximity to your house or work is paramount, or maybe you prefer a small clinic run by one or two doctors. Perhaps you like the idea of a big clinic with access to multiple doctors, or possibly a mobile veterinarian who makes house calls is more to your liking.

Finding the Right Veterinarian

Finding the right veterinarian is not difficult, but it can be a bit time consuming. The good news is the hard work you invest today will pay off in the future when you need to put your Border Collie's health and well being in the hands of a veterinarian.

To start your search:

- Ask the breeder of your Border Collie for a referral. Most reputable breeders know several local veterinarians and specialists.
- Ask friends, family, neighbors, and colleagues who own a pet for a referral.
- Ask around at local dog clubs, obedience schools, dog groomers, or boarding kennels. These people are usually involved in dogs and will have established a relationship with one or more local veterinarians.
- Local telephone directories are often a good starting point. They will give you the names, addresses, and telephone numbers of veterinary and emergency clinics in your area.
- If you are moving from one area to another, ask your current veterinarian to refer you to some veterinarians in your new town.
- Contact the American Animal Hospital Association (AAHA) for names of member veterinarians in your area.

Visiting the Clinic

This can be a bit time consuming, but, again, the time invested today will be well worth the effort down the road. You may feel less anxious if you see where your Border Collie will be spending the day if he needs to be hospitalized overnight or kept for several hours. When visiting veterinary clinics, don't be afraid to ask for a tour of their exam rooms, X-ray room, operating and recovery rooms, boarding areas, and so forth. If the clinic is busy or an emergency arises, you may need to schedule an appointment, which is not an unreasonable request. If the staff or veterinarians refuse to show you their facilities, run, don't walk, to the nearest exit.

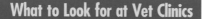

What to Look for at Vet Clinics

- Is the clinic neat and clean? Are there unpleasant odors?
- Are the exam rooms cleaned and disinfected between animals?
- Is the clinic organized? Does it run smoothly? Or is it noisy and chaotic?
- Is there a fenced or grassy area for pottying your Border Collie?
- Do you like the location? Is it conveniently located and easy for you to get to?
- Does the waiting area provide adequate room for separating large and small dogs, unruly dogs from nervous dogs, and rambunctious dogs from shy dogs?

Veterinarians, Staff, and Assistants

Like human doctors, veterinarians differ in their bedside manners. Regardless of the veterinarian's qualifications, if you do not like him/her or the staff, you will not be comfortable taking your Border Collie there. The relationship between you and your veterinarian can last for 10 to 15 years. Good communication with doctor and staff is a necessity.

- Are you comfortable talking with the veterinarian and asking questions?
- Does he/she seem knowledgeable and friendly?
- Is he/she patient? Willing to answer your questions? Responsive to your concerns?
- Does he/she explain the diagnosis, treatment, and expected outcome in layman's terms? Will that be explained again if you don't understand?
- Do you feel rushed?
- Is your Border Collie treated with kindness, respect, and concern?
- Is the staff knowledgeable, courteous, and friendly? Are they willing to answer your questions and accommodate reasonable requests? Or do they give you the brush off?

Of course, there is always the chance that your personality will differ or clash with a particular veterinarian despite his/her stellar academic qualifications. If this is the case, keep looking until you find the veterinarian that is right for you.

Your puppy's breeder may be able to help you find a trusted veterinarian.

Preparing for Emergencies

Anyone who has ever owned a dog knows that emergencies never happen between eight am and five pm. It's Murphy's Law with a twist. Anything that can go wrong will go wrong, and it will happen on weekends, holidays, and always after your veterinarian's office has just closed for the day. Therefore, it is always prudent to know the location of the closest emergency veterinary clinic. Emergency animal clinics handle emergencies that occur outside of your veterinarian's regular office hours. Most generally, they do not handle routine check-ups, vaccinations, or spaying and neutering. Emergency clinics may also see animals who need 24-hour care or exams with specialized equipment that the veterinarians in the surrounding area do not have at their facilities.

PREVENTATIVE CARE FOR YOUR BORDER COLLIE

Once you have found a veterinarian and are satisfied with your choice, it is time to get your Border Collie an appointment. Generally speaking, you will want to get your new pooch to the veterinarian within 48 to 72 hours after acquiring him. Many breeders recommend this because it establishes a record of health and helps detect any potential problems within the necessary time requirements established by the breeder's contract. To the untrained eye, a puppy or adult dog who appears healthy can still have a serious problem. One of the most important and kindest deeds you can do for your Border Collie is to work with a veterinarian to develop a preventive healthcare plan and schedule routine visits.

The Physical Exam

Your veterinarian will check your Border Collie's overall condition, which includes inspecting his skin, coat, eyes, ears, feet, lymph nodes, glands, teeth and gums. He/she will listen to his heart and lungs, and feel his abdomen, muscles, and joints. Most likely, he/she will ask you about your puppy's eating and elimination habits. If necessary, jot down any relevant information beforehand so you will have it at your fingertips, such as the type of food your puppy eats, how much and how often he eats, how often he relieves himself, the color, shape and size of his stools, and so forth. He/she will no doubt discuss with you a preventative healthcare plan that includes vaccinations, worming, spaying or neutering, and scheduling routine veterinary visits.

Annual Checkups

You may not feel older from one birthday to the next, but one year is a long time in your Border Collie's life. In a relatively short period of time, about ten to twelve years, your Border Collie will have grown from a tiny puppy to a senior citizen. Experts say one human year can be equivalent to seven to ten dog years, and in dog circles that means a lot can happen in the span of one year. Some veterinarians recommend bi-annual check-ups—especially for dogs over seven years of age. This may seem excessive, but remember in six short months your Border Collie will have aged the equivalent of three to five dog years.

It is not unusual for owners to inadvertently overlook their Border

Collie's health. Let's face it, how many people go to the doctor's unless they are feeling particularly ill? When your Border Collie is happy and healthy and full of zest, annual preventative healthcare visits can get overlooked.

However, it is important to schedule (and keep!) those yearly exams because diseases such as diabetes, kidney failure, arthritis, dental disease, and cancer can become more prevalent as your Border Collie ages.

VACCINATIONS

Vaccinations are really important for you Border Collie puppy. He needs to be properly socialized starting at a young age, and the sooner he starts his course of vaccinations, the sooner he will be able to get out and about and begin socializing with people and other animals and exploring his new world. A reputable breeder will most likely have administered a series of vaccinations for distemper, hepatitis, leptospirosis, parvovirus, and parainfluenza, prior to you acquiring your Border Collie.

Vaccinations generally start being administered at six to eight weeks of age and continue every three to four weeks until the puppy is sixteen weeks old. You should have received a copy of his vaccination and deworming schedule when you picked up your Border Collie puppy. It is a good idea to take a copy of your puppy's

All Border Collies should have an annual veterinary exam so their overall condition can be evaluated.

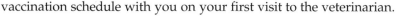

Why Spraying and Neutering Is a Good Idea.

Spaying or neutering your Border Collie will help reduce pet overpopulation and keep your pet healthy by preventing or eliminating a number of medical and behavior problems, including

- helps to reduce or eliminate breast cancer.

- ovarian and uterine infection or cancer.

- mammary gland tumors.

- can help to prevent nervousness, irritability, and aggressiveness that many females show while in season.

- eliminates the possibility of passing on genetic defects, such as hip dysplasia and epilepsy.

- eliminates a female's heat cycle and any possibility of an "accidental" breeding, resulting in unwanted puppies, which contribute to pet overpopulation problems.

- eliminates testicular cancer and decreases the incidence of prostate disease.

- helps to decrease aggression toward other male dogs, as well as people.

- decreases a dog's desire to "roam" the neighborhood, which in turn reduces the risk of fights, injury, poisoning, accidents, and diseases.

- increases ability to pay attention to their owners because they are not constantly distracted by females in season.

vaccination schedule with you on your first visit to the veterinarian. Your veterinarian will set up a continued vaccination schedule for your Border Collie, including a rabies vaccination at the appropriate time. Veterinarians differ on their vaccination protocol so it is important to ask questions, especially if you have any concerns.

Diseases to Vaccinate Against

The following is a list of viral and bacterial diseases that may be recommended for your Border Collie. Your veterinarian will help you make a decision that takes into account your lifestyle and the region in which you live.

- **Distemper:** A highly contagious viral disease very similar to the virus that causes measles in humans. Distemper is spread through the air as well as through contact with an infected animal's stool or urine. It is a primary cause of illness and death in unvaccinated puppies.

- **Hepatitis:** Also known as canine adenovirus, it typically affects the liver, tonsils, and larynx, but can also attack other organs in the body. The virus is spread primarily through direct contact with an infected dog and infected fluids including saliva, nasal discharge, and urine.

- **Kennel Cough:** Also known as canine infectious *tracheobronchitis* or *Bordetellosis*, it is normally characterized by a harsh, dry coughing or hacking, which may be followed by retching and gagging. The disease is airborne—meaning it is passed through the air—and can spread rapidly among dogs who live together.

- **Leptospirosis:** A bacterial disease that is transmitted primarily through the urine of infected animals. The disease can get into water or soil and can survive for weeks to months. Border Collies, as well as humans, can become infected through contact with the contaminated urine or the contaminated water or soil.

- **Lyme Disease:** A bacterial infection caused by a slender spiral microorganism identified as *Borrelia burgdorferi,* it is transmitted to humans and dogs through the bite of an infected deer tick, also known as the black-legged tick. If infection occurs, the spirochetes migrate, invade, and penetrate into connective tissues, skin joints, and the nervous system.

- **Parvovirus:** A deadly and highly contagious gastrointestinal disease that normally affects puppies more frequently than adult dogs. The majority of puppies infected are under six months of age, with the most severe cases seen in puppies younger than 12 weeks of age.

- **Rabies:** A viral disease that affects the brain and is almost invariably fatal once symptoms begin to appear. Transmission of the virus is almost always through a bite from a rabid animal. The virus is relatively slow moving with the average incubation time from exposure to brain involvement (in dogs) between three and eight weeks.

HEALTH ISSUES IN THE BORDER COLLIE

Border Collies, in general, are a pretty healthy breed with an average lifespan of around 13 years. However, like most breeds, the Border Collie is not immune to health problems, and genetic diseases remain of paramount importance to reputable breeders. Your Border Collie's life will be shaped, influenced, and prolonged by the excellent health care and daily companionship you provide. But sometimes, regardless of your meticulous attention and best efforts, a Border Collie, for whatever reason, will develop a health problem.

Just as you are a reflection of your parents' genetic contributions, your Border

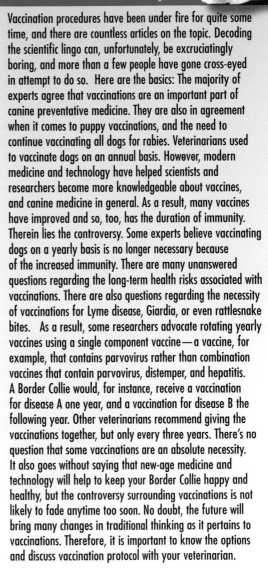

The Vaccination Controversy

Vaccination procedures have been under fire for quite some time, and there are countless articles on the topic. Decoding the scientific lingo can, unfortunately, be excruciatingly boring, and more than a few people have gone cross-eyed in attempt to do so. Here are the basics: The majority of experts agree that vaccinations are an important part of canine preventative medicine. They are also in agreement when it comes to puppy vaccinations, and the need to continue vaccinating all dogs for rabies. Veterinarians used to vaccinate dogs on an annual basis. However, modern medicine and technology have helped scientists and researchers become more knowledgeable about vaccines, and canine medicine in general. As a result, many vaccines have improved and so, too, has the duration of immunity. Therein lies the controversy. Some experts believe vaccinating dogs on a yearly basis is no longer necessary because of the increased immunity. There are many unanswered questions regarding the long-term health risks associated with vaccinations. There are also questions regarding the necessity of vaccinations for Lyme disease, Giardia, or even rattlesnake bites. As a result, some researchers advocate rotating yearly vaccines using a single component vaccine—a vaccine, for example, that contains parvovirus rather than combination vaccines that contain parvovirus, distemper, and hepatitis. A Border Collie would, for instance, receive a vaccination for disease A one year, and a vaccination for disease B the following year. Other veterinarians recommend giving the vaccinations together, but only every three years. There's no question that some vaccinations are an absolute necessity. It also goes without saying that new-age medicine and technology will help to keep your Border Collie happy and healthy, but the controversy surrounding vaccinations is not likely to fade anytime too soon. No doubt, the future will bring many changes in traditional thinking as it pertains to vaccinations. Therefore, it is important to know the options and discuss vaccination protocol with your veterinarian.

Collie is the sum of his genetic makeup that he inherited from his relatives—primarily his parents and grandparents. These genes lay the foundation for his size, markings, structure, temperament, work ethic, and overall health.

The genetic problems that are of primary concern to Border Collie breeders and owners include collie eye anomaly, epilepsy (idiopathic), and hip dysplasia.

Collie Eye Anomaly

Originally discovered in Collies, Collie eye anomaly (CEA) is an inherited disease. While it has been well studied in other breeds, the genetics of CEA in Border Collies has not been conclusively established. What experts do know is CEA is a defect in the formation of the eye. More specifically, it is a defect in the formation of the blood vessels and adjacent tissues underlying the retina, causing various eye abnormalities. CEA is caused by a single recessive gene, meaning a puppy who inherits one copy of the CEA gene from his mother and one copy from his father will have symptoms of the disease from birth. If he inherits a copy of the CEA gene from only one parent, he will be a *carrier* of the disease but will not show symptoms.

In most cases, an afflicted dog will have pits or notchlike defects in one or both eyes that affect the retina and adjacent tissues. Vision is always impaired, but the extent of impairment depends on the severity of the problem. Some dogs may have limited visual impairment and continue to function quite well. Others will be

Vaccinations are intended to safeguard your dog's health. Talk to your veterinarian about those your dog needs.

blind. In more severe cases, dogs may have a detached retina, optic nerve abnormalities, and loss of retinal cells. The onset of CEA occurs between three and eight weeks of age and is diagnosed on examination by a canine ophthalmologist.

There is no treatment for dogs with CEA. Most affected dogs have functional vision and can live relatively happy and productive lives. However, affected dogs should not be bred.

Epilepsy (Idiopathic)

Epilepsy is a term used to describe a disorder of recurring seizures. It is further characterized as *primary* or *secondary* epilepsy. Secondary epilepsy, also known as acquired or symptomatic epilepsy, refers to seizures for which a cause can be determined. It is secondary to some kind of brain damage that can be identified, such as a stroke, tumor, trauma, metabolic disease, congenital defect, or infection.

Primary epilepsy, also known as *idiopathic* epilepsy, refers to recurrent seizures that are of unknown cause. Simply put, veterinarians and researchers do not know what triggers the seizures. Experts say, "the only thing predictable about idiopathic epilepsy is that it is unpredictable."

Idiopathic epilepsy is of primary concern to breeders and owners because it is considered one of the most common neurologic diseases in dogs, and it is a genetic disease known to affect Border Collies. While there is a strong indication of genetic inheritance, the exact mode of inheritance is not yet known.

Diagnosis and Treatment

There are no tests that can give a definitive diagnosis of epilepsy. Diagnosis is made by ruling out every other possibility. Dogs with epilepsy often have normal laboratory findings, so veterinarians will perform a physical examination and carefully review the dog's medical history and, if available, his seizure history. Dogs with idiopathic epilepsy usually have their first seizure between one and five years of age.

Canine idiopathic epilepsy is a chronic disease, and there is no cure. Treatment usually involves anti-epileptic drug therapy, such as phenobarbital, diazepam, and potassium bromide to decrease the frequency, severity, and duration of the seizures.

Tidbit

Keep track of your dog's worming, flea, and vaccination schedule on a calendar or journal that you look at frequently. Write down the dates he was treated, and then flip ahead and jot down the dates he is due for another treatment. Not all veterinarians send reminders, and more than a few get lost in the mail.

Evaluation of hips done by the OFA are categorized and graded as:

- Normal (Excellent, Good, Fair)
- Borderline
- Dysplastic (Mild, Moderate, Severe)

Hip Dysplasia

Hip dysplasia is one of the most common heritable orthopedic diseases in dogs. *Dysplasia* means a developmental abnormality, which can include size, shape, or formation. Hip dysplasia is a defect in the conformation of the hip joint that can cause weakness and lameness to a dog's rear quarters, resulting in arthritis, severe debilitating pain, and crippling. The resulting arthritis is frequently referred to as *degenerative joint disease*, *arthrosis*, or *osteoarthritis*.

While it is known to affect mostly giant and large breed dogs, hip dysplasia can occur, albeit rarely, in medium-sized and even small breeds. It is important to breeders and owners because it affects Border Collies, too.

Symptoms

Symptoms of hip dysplasia vary, making it difficult, if not impossible, to predict when or even if a dysplastic Border Collie will show symptoms. Some Border Collies are very stoic and will continue working regardless of the pain. Caloric intake, level of exercise, weather, and other environmental influences can influence the appearance of symptoms. Some dysplastic dogs still remain active, while others exhibit severe lameness.

The symptoms associated with hip dysplasia are not unlike the symptoms associated with other causes of arthritis. Some dogs may experience a decrease in activity. They may walk or run with an altered gait and will frequently resist movements requiring full extension or flexion of the rear legs. Some Border Collies may experience stiffness and pain in their rear legs after exercise or first thing in the morning upon arising. They may have difficulty rising from a lying or sitting position and may balk at using stairs. Other dogs may have a swaying, unsteady gait or a "bunny hop" gait where they run with both hind legs moving together.

Diagnosis

A preliminary diagnosis of hip dysplasia can be made through a combination of physical examinations and x-rays, and by ruling out other problems such as hip and spine disorders, ruptured cruciate ligament, Lyme disease, and so forth. For a definitive evaluation, x-rays can be submitted to the Orthopedic Foundation for Animals (OFA) where three radiologists evaluate the hip joint and a consensus score is assigned.

Treatment

Treatment of hip dysplasia varies and can include over-the-counter drugs like nutraceuticals such as glucosamine, chondroitin, and methylsulfonylmethane (MSM), or buffered aspirin. Your veterinarian may also prescribe a pain reliever. Depending on the age of your Border Collie and the severity of joint degeneration, your veterinarian may recommend surgery, which can include a femoral head ostectomy, triple pelvic osteotomy, or, in some cases, a total hip replacement.

COMMON CANINE HEALTH PROBLEMS

Common canine health problems that are found in most breeds of dogs and may be present in some Border Collies are not considered to be a significant health concern in the Border Collie breed. These include anterior cruciate ligament ruptures (ACL), cataracts, elbow disease, focal/multifocal acquired retinopathy (FMAR), and progressive retinal atrophy (PRA).

Anterior Cruciate Ligament (ACL)

No doubt you have heard of athletes who injure or "blow out" their knees. These types of injuries are usually a result of a specific trauma. Dogs too are susceptible to knee injuries, such as the commonly seen ruptured anterior cruciate ligament, but many are attributed less to a specific trauma and more to a gradual degeneration of the ligament.

A dog's *stifle* (knee) joint is formed by three bones: the *femur*, the long bone extending down from the hip; the

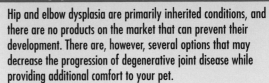

Tips for Coping With Hip or Elbow Dysplasia

Hip and elbow dysplasia are primarily inherited conditions, and there are no products on the market that can prevent their development. There are, however, several options that may decrease the progression of degenerative joint disease while providing additional comfort to your pet.

● Weight management is the first step and one of the most important things you can do for your dysplastic Border Collie's overall health. Extra pounds put additional stress on his already compromised joints, and an overweight Border Collie is more susceptible to injuries. If necessary, seek veterinary assistance on the appropriate amount and type of food to feed.

● Exercise your dog regularly, but not to excess. Your veterinarian can help you design an exercise program that is best suited for your dog based on his overall health, weight, and joint condition. Choose an exercise that provides good range of motion while limiting wear and tear on the joints, such as walking on surfaces with good traction, or swimming. Avoid retrieving games where a dog is jumping, which is hard on the joints and can exacerbate problems.

● Whether your Border Collie is young or old, he is sure to appreciate a warm, comfortable place for sleeping. Orthopedic beds are ideal and provide the necessary cushioning for dogs with sore joints. Equally important, dogs with aches and pains will be able to get on and off an orthopedic bed much easier than other types of soft, fluffy beds. Be sure the bed is placed in a warm spot away from drafts.

● Like people, dogs love a good massage to help relax his muscles and promote a good range of motion in his joints! Consider regular visits to a canine chiropractor or physical therapist, or ask an expert to show you how to massage your dog. As with most dog-related activities, it is always best to start slow. If your Border Collie is in pain, you do not want to risk aggravating the situation.

● For dogs with moderate amounts of pain or lameness, consider building or purchasing a ramp so your Border Collie does not need to maneuver steps or stairs. In some cases, stairs or steps may be enough to prevent your dog from getting outside to urinate or defecate.

This dog appears to have healthy eyes, but Collie eye anomaly (CEA) is a concern in Border Collies.

tibia the bone between the knee and ankle; and the *patella,* the kneecap. These bones are joined together by a number of muscles and ligaments. Unlike the hip and elbow joints, which are designed to prevent excess or abnormal movement, a dog's knee joint has no interlocking bones. Instead, it must rely solely on the soft tissue structures in and around the joint to hold it in place and protect it from injury.

The *anterior* (forward) *cruciate ligament* and the *posterior* (rear) *cruciate ligament* crisscross, forming an X in the knee joint and keeping the femur and tibia from moving back and forth across each other. The anterior cruciate ligament, which provides the most stability to the knee during weight bearing, is the ligament that tends to rupture. When there is a partial or complete tear, the knee's stability is severely weakened, which in turn causes joint inflammation and damage.

Cause

Here's where it gets a bit tricky—the cause of the tearing is generally unknown. Many experts believe that the excessive release of degradative enzymes in the tissue of the knee joint degrades the collagen within the ligament and weakens the ACL, predisposing it to rupture. A dog who twists on his hind leg, slips on a slippery surface, or makes a sudden or fast turn while running can rupture his cruciate ligament. Because of the non-traumatic nature of torn ACLs, there is a significant chance—some experts suggest between 30 and 80 percent—that the opposite ACL will also tear.

Equally important, obesity puts additional weight on the knee and overweight Border Collies tend to have more occurrences of ruptured ACLs than their lean counterparts.

Symptoms can occur suddenly or gradually, and include stiffness or limping in the dog's hind leg, particularly after exercise or prolonged periods of rest. It is not uncommon for the limping to become progressively worse over time. Some dogs will sit with their hind leg off to one side. Other dogs may have an intermittent clicking noise when walking.

Diagnosis and Treatment

As with other orthopedic problems, diagnosis usually involves a physical examination, manipulation of the joint, and observation of joint movement. A definitive diagnosis can be made with the help of X-rays. Surgery is the generally the most common method of correction. The longer the knee goes untreated, the greater the chance of irreversible arthritic conditions developing.

Elbow Disease

Anatomically, a dog's elbow joint is similar to a human's elbow. It is a complicated hinge-type joint that is created by the junction of three different bones: the *ulna*, *radius*, and *humerus*. These bones fit and function together with little room for error and all the parts must work harmoniously for maximum soundness and efficiency. Any alteration in the elbow configuration will affect a dog's ability to use his leg correctly.

Elbow disease—frequently referred to as *elbow dysplasia* or *elbow incongruency*—is really a syndrome for different elbow abnormalities

Hip dysplasia affects many breeds of dogs; the hard-working Border Collie is also a candidate.

like *ununited anconeal process* (UAP), *fragmented medial coronoid process* (FCP), and *osteochondritis dessicans* (OCD). What makes elbow disease so frustrating is that a dog can develop an elbow problem that eventually causes further problems, or the dog may develop additional elbow problems independently because of genetic predispositions.

Symptoms

Symptoms of all three elbow diseases are similar and can include a weight-bearing lameness in the front legs that persists for more than a few days, reduction in range of movement, and pain when a veterinarian manipulates the joint. The next diagnostic step usually includes a set of high quality x-rays. In some instances, a CT scan or exploratory surgery may be necessary to establish a definitive diagnosis. Depending on where you live, you may need to travel to a veterinary teaching hospital or specialized clinic.

Treatment

Treatment varies, depending on the diagnosis. With FCP and OCD, many experts first recommend medical treatment, which includes a specifically designed exercise program, weight loss, if necessary, and the use of nutraceuticals such as glucosamine and chondroitin, as well as non-steroidal anti-inflammatory medications. In some instances of FCP and OCD, surgery may be necessary. UAP is generally treated with surgery.

Focal/Multifocal Acquired Retinopathy (FMAR)

One of the most frequently seen retinal lesions in Border Collies—especially hard-working herding dogs—FMAR is characterized by bull's-eye type lesions in the retina that can accumulate over several years, leading to impaired vision and sometimes blindness. FMAR lesions are sometimes mistaken for Progressive Retinal Atrophy, especially in the later stages of the disease.

The dog's age at the onset of lesions, their rate of accumulation, and progression vary from dog to dog. Characteristically, males are affected more often than females, and the lesions are asymmetrical—meaning one eye is affected more than the other. The nature of the disease strongly suggests an environmental cause rather than an inherited cause, which makes controlling, preventing, and treating the disease difficult.

Progressive Retinal Atrophy

Progressive retinal atrophy (PRA) is the name for several inherited progressive diseases that lead to blindness. A dog's retina contains photoreceptors called *cones* and *rods*. Cones help a dog see at night or in darkness, while the rods allow a dog to see certain colors. Normally, the photoreceptors in the retina develop after birth to about eight weeks of age. Retinas of dogs with PRA either have arrested development (*retinal dysplasia*) or early photoreceptor degeneration. A comparable disease in humans is retinitis pigmentosa.

PRA worsens over time with affected dogs generally experiencing night blindness first. Eventually, the condition progresses to failed daytime vision. Unfortunately, there is no treatment for PRA.

DEALING WITH PARASITES

Parasites. They sound grotesque and to the average dog owner, they usually are. Unfortunately, it is highly likely that sometime within your Border Collie's life he will suffer from an internal parasite (like worms) or an external one (like fleas). Both types of parasites need treatment. Left unchecked, parasites can cause debilitating and life-threatening problems.

External Parasites

Fleas and ticks can wreak havoc with your Border Collie. Keeping one step ahead of these annoying parasites will keep your canine companion happy, healthy, and comfortable.

Fleas

If you own a Border Collie, you no doubt know a thing or two about fleas! One bite from these pesky creatures can cause itching for days. And where there is one flea, it is a safe bet there are plenty more looming in your carpet, furniture, bedding, and on your precious Border Collie! What you may not know is there are over 2,200 species of fleas worldwide.

Flea Allergy Dermatitis

If your Border Collie is sensitive to fleas, one bite from this tiny, nearly invisible pest can make his life (and yours!) miserable and plunge him into a vicious cycle of biting, scratching, and licking. Flea allergy dermatitis, also known as bite hypersensitivity, tends to be most prevalent during the summer when fleas are most rampant and annoying.

Fleas feeding on your Border Collie inject saliva that contains different antigens and histamine-like substances, resulting in irritation and itching sensations that can range from mild to downright nasty. Dogs with flea allergies may itch over their entire bodies, experience generalized hair loss, and develop red, inflamed skin and hot spots. They are frequently restless and uncomfortable, and may spend a great deal of their time scratching, digging, licking, and chewing their skin.

Treatments vary and can be multi-faceted. Of primary importance is a strict flea control program to prevent additional infestation. Veterinarians frequently recommend hypoallergenic or colloidal oatmeal-type shampoos to remove allergens, and topical anti-itch creams to soothe the skin. These products usually provide immediate, short-term relief, but are not a long-term solution. Additionally, fatty acid supplements, such as Omega-3 and Omega-6, which are found in flaxseed and fish oils, are proving helpful in reducing the amount and effects of histamine. In some cases, veterinarians may prescribe corticosteroids to reduce itching.

In North America, only a few species of fleas commonly infest dogs. The *Ctenocephalides felis*, also known as the domestic cat flea, likes both cats and dogs, and is the most common flea responsible for wreaking havoc with your Border Collie. A flea is about one-eighth inch long, slightly smaller than a sesame seed, and generally brown or black in color. They are wingless bloodsuckers that are responsible for spreading tapeworms to dogs and causing serious allergy dermatitis. In serious infestations, fleas can cause anemia, especially in puppies.

Getting Rid of Fleas

The advent of once-a-month topical treatments makes eradicating fleas a lot easier than it was ten or fifteen years ago. But you still need to keep on top of the pesky buggers. If you live where the temperature freezes, count your blessings. The cat flea is susceptible to cold, and no life stage of the flea can survive when exposed to temperatures below roughly 37 degrees Fahrenheit (3 degrees Celsius).

To control and eliminate fleas, try these steps:

- Clean everything your dog has come in contact with. Wash his dog beds and blankets and mop up floors. Vacuum all carpets, rugs, and furniture. Immediately dispose of vacuum bags because eggs can hatch in them.
- If necessary, remove dense vegetation near your home, dog yard, or kennel area—these spaces offer a damp microenvironment that is favorable to flea development.
- Treat your Border Collie and any other household pets who can serve as hosts, such as other dogs, cats, and ferrets.

Dogs who spend a lot of time outdoors are particularly liable to pick up external parasites like ticks and fleas.

- A number of insecticides and insect growth regulators are available for use in the home and have proven effective. However, it is worth noting that some insecticides are toxic. It is important to read all labels and follow directions carefully.
- There are also a number of on-animal flea control products, such as shampoos, sprays, dips, powders, and flea collars. Many of these products have been around for years, but, again, it is important to remember that many commercial and natural products may be toxic. They may irritate your Border Collie's skin or cause health problems.

Ticks

Unlike fleas, which are insects with six legs, ticks have eight legs, like mites and spiders. There are approximately 850 species of these blood-sucking parasites that burrow into your Border Collie's skin and engorge themselves with blood, expanding to many times their size. They are dangerous because they can secrete a paralysis-causing toxin and can spread serious diseases such as Lyme disease, Rocky Mountain spotted fever, Texas fever, tularemia, babesiosis, and canine ehrlichiosis. It is not unusual for a tick to be infected with and transmit more than one disease. Therefore, it is not at all uncommon to see a dog infected with more than one disease at a time. In severe infestations, anemia and even death may occur

Your Border Collie is most likely to pick up ticks in wooded areas, grassy areas, and overgrown fields. Ticks commonly imbed themselves between the toes, in the ears, and around the neck but can be found elsewhere on the body. Each species has its own favored feeding sites on your Border Collie.

Controlling ticks on your Border Collie is not unlike the process for flea control. You must be committed and diligent. You will want to treat your yard, house, doghouse, dog blankets, and your dog with products specifically designed for ticks. There are a number of

How to Safely Remove a Tick

Removing an attached tick is not terribly difficult—once you get past any queasiness about doing so.

- Always use a pair of tweezers or a specially designed tick-removing tool. Small curved hemostats or curved tip jeweler tweezers also work well.
- Grasp the tick as close as possible to where it enters your dog's skin.
- Pull slowly, firmly, and steadily in an outward direction. Don't jerk, squeeze, or twist the tick.
- After removing the tick, place it in a jar of alcohol to kill it. Some experts recommend keeping the tick alive in a sealed, dated vial for at least one month in case symptoms of tick-borne diseases develop. You can discuss this option with your veterinarian.
- It is not unusual for a small welt or skin reaction to occur once a tick is removed. Clean the bite wound with a disinfectant. If you want, apply an antibiotic ointment.

If you simply cannot bring yourself to remove a tick, take the dog to your veterinarian. Ticks must be removed, and the sooner the better.

over-the-counter products available such as sprays, foggers, powders, dips, shampoos, and collars. Once a month, topical ointments also are available. Unlike fleas, ticks are not susceptible to cold weather, so you will need to treat your yard late into the fall and early winter. Again, many of these products may be toxic. It is important to read all labels and follow directions carefully. When in doubt, consult your veterinarian before purchasing and using any tick control product. Your local university or health department should be able to provide you with information on the types of ticks found in your area, and their peak seasons. When taking your Border Collie for a walk, do not allow him to wander off designated paths or near low overhanging branches and shrubs where ticks are likely to be waiting for an unsuspecting Border Collie to pass by.

Life Threatening Symptoms

If your dog has any of these symptoms, seek medical assistance right away:

- Bleeding that is heavy or can't be stopped
- Breathing that is difficult, labored, or no breathing at all
- Collapse, coma, depression, extreme lethargy, or unconsciousness
- Diarrhea—uncontrolled, bloody or stools that are black and tarry
- Gums that are bluish or white
- Lethargy
- No pulse or heart beat
- Pain
- Seizures
- Temperature over 105 degrees F (normal is less than 102.5)
- Vomiting blood or uncontrolled vomiting

Seek immediate veterinary assistance if your dog has been exposed to trauma, poisoning, or gastrointestinal distress including:

- Bite from a snake, poisonous spider, or another animal—especially a cat or unvaccinated animal
- Electrocution (i.e., chewing on an electrical cord)
- Excessive heat or cold
- Head trauma of any kind
- Overdose of medications
- Poisoning—including foods, nicotine, chemicals, toxins, medications, etc.
- Porcupine quills embedded in the skin
- Puncture wounds
- Trauma of any kind—hit by a car, kicked by a horse, falling from an open window, the bed of a pickup, balcony, etc.
- Swallowing a foreign object (toy, marble, paperclip, sock, etc)
- Teeth that are broken, bleeding, or loose

This is a small sampling of the things that can go wrong when you own a Border Collie. When in doubt, it is always prudent to seek veterinary attention right away.

Internal Parasites

Internal parasites are called endoparasites becuase they live inside your Border Collie's body. The most common are heartworms, hookworms, roundworms, tapeworms, and whipworms. There are a number of deworming medications available at local pet stores and retail outlets. However, dewormers differ drastically in their safety and effectiveness in expelling worms from the body. Therefore, the wise choice is to have a veterinarian diagnose the specific type of internal parasite and then prescribe the proper deworming medication.

- **Heartworms:** Found throughout the United States, they are potentially the most dangerous internal parasites. Mosquitoes transmit the disease when they suck blood from an infected dog and then bite a healthy dog, thereby depositing larvae. The larvae grow inside the healthy dog, migrating through the dog's tissues into the bloodstream, and eventually into the dog's heart. The larvae grow into adult worms. Preventative medications are available and are highly recommended. However, they must never be given to a dog who is already infected with adult worms.

For an alternate method of prevention and cure of common problems, you may want to explore and use alternative remedies.

Therefore, it is imperative that you consult with your veterinarian before starting any preventative treatment for heartworms.

- **Hookworms:** They can cause diarrhea, vomiting, and life-threatening anemia. A Border Collie's gums may appear pale, the dog may be weak, and sometimes black, tarry stools can be seen. Hookworms are contracted either through a dog's mother or through contaminated soil and feces, which makes sanitary practices paramount. All fecal material should be removed daily. When walking in public places, do not allow your dog to come in contact with other dogs' feces.
- **Roundworms:** Most puppies are born with roundworms—this is why most puppies require deworming at an early age. In more severe infestations, dogs may be thin and have a pot-bellied appearance. Their coats may be dry, dull, and rough looking. Some puppies may have intestinal discomfort and may cry as a result. Diarrhea or constipation and vomiting are also frequent symptoms. In some cases, a cough may develop due to the migration of the larvae through the respiratory system.
- **Tapeworms:** These worms generally do not cause any symptoms, although diarrhea may be present. Getting rid of tapeworms can be difficult because you must successfully eliminate the head of the tapeworm, otherwise it will regrow a new body. Flea and lice control are essential, otherwise your Border Collie will continue to reinfest himself.

•**Whipworms:** Dogs become infected when they ingest food or water that is contaminated with whipworm eggs. The symptoms vary depending on the number of worms in a dog's stomach. Often, mild infestations produce no obvious symptoms in healthy individuals. Larger infestations, however, have more pronounced symptoms and can result in inflammation of the intestinal wall. Anemia is possible if hemorrhaging into the intestine occurs. Some dogs may experience diarrhea, mucus, and blood in the stools, and weight loss. Like roundworms, soil contamination is an enormous problem. To help reduce or prevent contamination, fecal matter should be picked up daily and kennel or dog run areas cleaned thoroughly, and if possible, be allowed to dry in direct sunlight.

ALTERNATIVE MEDICINE

Alternative medicine is a term used to broadly describe methods and practices of medicine that are used in place of or in addition to conventional medical treatments. Traditional medicine is rooted in science, physics, chemistry, and biology, and its practices are backed by scientific data. While some alternative medicine has been around for thousands of years, it is empirical, meaning the evidence comes less from clinical trials and more from the anecdotes and testimonials of veterinarians and dog owners. As the demand for alternative medicine for humans has grown, so to has the demand for alternative veterinary medicine, which is sometimes referred to as Complementary and Alternative Veterinary Medicine (CAVM).

Alternative medicine encompasses a broad range of treatments including:

• Acupuncture
• Chiropractic
• Massage
• Herb, Natural Supplements, and Vitamin and Mineral Supplementation
• Homeopathy

The American Veterinary Medical Association has established guidelines for veterinary acupuncture, chiropractic, homeopathic, and holistic medicine. It is worth mentioning, that *alternative* and *herbal* do not mean harmless. The Food and Drug Administration (FDA) does not regulate herbs and natural supplements. They can cause side effects or result in cross-reactions if combined with other supplements or medications. To prevent problems, always consult your veterinarian.

FIRST AID AND EMERGENCY CARE

Dogs have the uncanny ability to get into anything and everything—usually at the most inopportune and unexpected times! If your dog is sick or injured, it is always best to err on the side of caution and contact your veterinarian or 24-hour emergency clinic right away. Many minor situations, such as scrapes, nicks, abrasions, or a bout of diarrhea, can be successfully treated at home, coupled with a "wait and see" attitude. It is imperative, however, that you be able to recognize the difference between a minor situation and a life-threatening medical emergency.

What's in a First-aid Kit?

First aid kits can vary in their content. Some specialty kits contain enough medical paraphernalia to perform minor surgeries. There are also mini first aid kits that clip on your belt for walks in the park, hiking, etc. Home kits contain basic first aid equipment. Whether you choose to purchase a super colossal pre-assembled kit, a basic home kit, or customize your own, it should contain basic necessities including:

- Activated charcoal (available from pharmacists; it binds or neutralizes certain poisons)
- Alcohol or alcohol prep pads (for sterilizing scissors, tweezers; not for use on wounds)
- Anti-diarrheal medicine
- Aspirin (not anti-inflammatory drugs)
- Ear cleaning solution
- Eye wash or saline solution (for flushing out eye contaminants)
- Eye ointment
- Gauze rolls and gauze pads
- Gloves (disposable latex for protecting hands, prevent contamination of wounds)
- Hydrogen peroxide 3% USP
- Important telephone numbers
- Instant cold pack
- Instant heat wrap
- Iodine (for cleaning wounds)

- Ipecac (to induce vomiting, if necessary)
- Lubricant (mineral oil or KY Jelly)
- Muzzle (a dog may try to bite if he is injured or scared)
- Ointments (triple antibiotic ointment inhibits bacterial growth in cuts, abrasions)
- Pill gun (for administering pills)
- Rehydrating solutions (i.e., Pedialyte or Gatorade to replace lost electrolytes)
- Scissors (to clip hair around wounds, cut gauze, etc.)
- Styptic pencil (stops bleeding if a nail is broken, torn, clipped too short)
- Thermometer (preferably digital)
- Tick removing tool
- Towels
- Turkey baster, bulb syringe, or large medical syringe (for flushing wounds)
- Tweezers
- Wraps (self-clinging, flexible elastic-type bandages for wrapping injuries)

How to Check for Dehydration

Dogs with diarrhea are susceptible to dehydration, so you will want to keep a close eye on your Border Collie. To check for dehydration, lift the skin at the scruff of his neck between your thumb and index finger, and pull it up an inch or so. Hold it there for a few seconds and let it go. Watch to see how long it takes for the skin to return to its normal position. If your dog is not dehydrated, the skin will spring back quickly and flatten out. If he is dehydrated, the skin will stay in a little ridge and take a few seconds to flatten out. If the skin does not flatten out at all and remains looking like a tent, your dog has an extreme medical emergency. You should seek veterinary attention right away.

You can also examine your Border Collie's gums. They should be a healthy pinkish color and moist. If your dog's gums are pale in color and dry, you should contact your veterinarian.

Choking

Dogs can choke on any number of items from disemboweled doll parts to buttons to safety pins to dog bones. Some Border Collies choke on their food if they wolf it down too quickly. Any obstruction of your dog's airway is a life-threatening medical emergency and must be dealt with immediately to prevent brain damage or death.

The symptoms of choking vary; however, the most common signs include a coughing, a gagging or retching noise, and pawing at the side of the face. His tongue may turn blue, and he may collapse. If you suspect your dog is choking, do not wait until the dog collapses to get help.

If possible, pull your Border Collie's lower jaw open and tilt his head upward. If an object is visible, try to remove it with your finger without pushing it deeper. It goes without saying that you should use extreme caution to avoid being bitten. Regardless of how friendly your dog might be, a panicked, choking dog is likely to bite as a reflex mechanism.

If the object cannot be removed easily, there is a Heimlich-type maneuver for dogs, not unlike the one used on humans. It is highly advisable that you become familiar with the procedure before a medical emergency arises. Your veterinarian can show you how to perform the procedure. For an adult or large dog: hold your dog from behind, wrap your arms around his body just behind the ribs. Wrap one hand around the other to make a double fist, placing the double fist on his abdomen below the rib cage. Squeeze sharply a few times, quickly pressing upward and forward until the object is expelled or dislodged.

For puppies: follow the above procedure, but rather than use a double fist, place the index and middle fingers of both hands on the puppy's abdomen below the rib cage. Press into the abdomen with a quick, upward thrust. It may take several tries to dislodge or expel the object. Once you have cleared your dog's airway, have him examined by a veterinarian as soon as possible.

Diarrhea

Diarrhea can occur if you overfeed your dog, if you change his normal food from one brand to another too quickly, or if there is a change in water while traveling. (That's why it is always prudent to carry your own water or purchase bottled water.) Unclean feeding bowls, stress, and allergies can also cause diarrhea. It can also be a

Regular – but not excessive – exercise and play will keep your Border Collie limber and less prone to injury.

symptom of intestinal parasites or disease.

Normal feces vary in color and consistency depending on the individual dog and his diet. Normal color usually ranges from light brown to dark brown. If the diarrhea is slight and your dog has no other symptoms, it may be nothing more than minor gastric upset. Withholding food for 24 hours, and then feeding a mixture of cooked white rice and extra lean hamburger browned in a skillet with any excess grease removed, may correct the problem. Medications such as Pepto-Bismol or Kaopectate every four hours may also fix the problem. It is always wise to consult your veterinarian before giving any human medications to your dog. He/she will be able to give you the correct dosage, as well. If you have a puppy or older dog with diarrhea or if the diarrhea is black or green, or your dog is showing other signs of illness, call your veterinarian right away.

Electrical Shock

If your puppy chews through the rubber coating of an electrical cord, chances are high he will receive an electrical shock. You may hear your dog yelp or cry out. However, if you are not around when it happens, you may notice symptoms that include severe burns in your puppy's mouth—especially the roof and tongue areas. The areas will be red and irritated, which may take several days as the burned tissue dies. In severe cases, the electrical current may travel into your puppy's body, causing damage to his lungs, which may result in death if left untreated. Symptoms of damaged lungs may include difficulty breathing, as a result of fluid accumulating in the lungs. In all cases of electrical shock—even cases of suspected electrical shock—always seek veterinary care.

Heat-Induced Illnesses

The average body temperature of a dog is 101.5 degrees Fahrenheit (38.6 degrees Celsius), with a normal range between 100 and 102 degrees Fahrenheit (37 and 39 degrees Celsius). These are core temperatures based on rectal thermometer readings. While temperatures can vary throughout a dog's body, the core temperature is what a dog's body uses to maintain constant internal (homeostatic) conditions, and includes blood pressure, blood chemistry, and body temperature. Heat-induced illnesses occur when a dog's normal body mechanisms cannot keep his temperature within a safe range.

Unlike humans, dogs do not sweat. Their primary cooling mechanisms are panting and conduction. When overheated dogs pant, they breathe in and out through their mouths. They inhale cool air and as the air moves into their lungs it absorbs heat and moisture. When they exhale, the hot air passes over their wet tongues and evaporation occurs, which helps to enhance and maximize heat loss and cool their bodies.

Conduction, the second method of cooling, occurs when a dog lies down on a cool surface, such as a tile floor, grass, or wet concrete. The coolness of the surface is transferred to his body through his relatively hairless tummy coming in contact with the cool surface.

There are four types of heat-induced illnesses: heat cramps, heat exhaustion, heat prostration, and heatstroke. Heat cramps are muscle cramps that are caused by the loss of salt from a dog's system and by extreme exertion in hot weather. Heat cramps do not normally occur in dogs, and it is highly unlikely you will encounter them in a Border Collie. The specific heat related health issues

In Case of an Emergency

Prevention is always the best route. However, in spite of your best intentions, accidents do happen. Therefore, it is prudent to familiarize yourself with the various emergency response protocols. A number of canine first aid books and videos are available through retail outlets and online. If possible, attend a canine first aid seminar and have a canine first aid kit on hand. You can purchase pre-assembled kits or assemble your own. Equally important, you should post in a conspicuous spot the following numbers:

- ASPCA Poison Control Hotline 1-888-426-4435 (there is a fee, which is charged to your credit card)

- Your veterinarian's number

- A 24-hour emergency veterinary clinic (in the event your vet's office is closed)

- The local animal control office in case your dog is lost

When calling the Poison Control Hotline, you will want to provide the following information: the type of poison ingested, the amount, and the duration since ingestion, and any symptoms your dog is experiencing. You will also need your Border Collie's age, sex, and weight.

that you should be aware of are heat exhaustion, heat prostration, and heatstroke.

- **Heat Exhaustion:** The least severe of the heat-related illnesses; however, it should still be taken seriously. It is characterized by lethargy and an inability to perform normal activities or work, such as obedience, agility, or tracking because of extreme heat.
- **Heat Prostration:** Heat prostration is the next level of seriousness, with a dog's body temperature around 104 to 106 degrees Fahrenheit (40 to 41 degrees Celsius). Possible signs would include rapid panting, red or pale gums, weakness, vomiting, mental confusion, and dizziness. You should not delay in seeking immediate veterinary attention.
- **Heatstroke:** Occurs when a dog's body temperatures is over 106 degrees Fahrenheit (41 degrees Celsius). Dogs suffering from heatstroke will display signs that include rapid panting, collapsing, inability to stand up, red or pale gums, thick and sticky saliva, weakness, vomiting (with or without blood), diarrhea, shock, fainting, or a coma. At this stage, it is a life threatening medical emergency that can result in multiple organ system dysfunction including the respiratory, cardiovascular, gastrointestinal, renal, and central nervous systems. Immediate veterinary assistance is essential.

Try to be patient with your ailing Border Collie, and consider using medications that could ease his senior symptoms.

What Should You Do?

The best defense against heat-related illnesses is to monitor your dog and his activities and do not place him in a situation where he can become overheated. For instance, limit exercise, such as running, playing, herding, training, etc., to the cooler parts of the day. If your dog is experiencing symptoms of heatstroke, get him to a cool environment immediately. Lower his temperature by submerging his body in cool (not cold) water, keeping his head elevated above the water, or applying cool water to his body with a shower or hose. If he will drink on his own, give him water or a rehydrating solution. Do not force water down his gullet, as he is likely to choke. Place him on a wet towel to keep him cool, and get medical assistance immediately.

Poisoning

So goes the saying, "an ounce of prevention…" But accidents do happen, and if you suspect your dog has come in contact with a poisonous substance, you should treat it as a medical emergency. Do not delay—seek immediate veterinary attention. If you see your dog eating or drinking a poisonous substance, do not wait for symptoms to develop. Call the Poison Control Center or take your dog to the nearest veterinary clinic. Do not induce vomiting unless instructed by a veterinarian.

Seniors are truly living their golden years. It's up to you to make them as comfortable as possible.

Treatment varies depending on the type of poison ingested. Therefore, it is important to take with you, if possible, the remains of the toxic product, be it a half-eaten plant, a mangled snail bait package, or a half-eaten box of chocolates. If your dog has vomited, scoop up the remains and take it with you. It can provide the veterinarian with important clues regarding the type of poison your dog ingested.

Vomiting

It is not unusual for dogs to vomit occasionally, and they can do so with little discomfort. Dogs vomit when they get excited, drink too much water too fast (especially after exercise), gulp their food, when they go for a ride in the car, or after they've eaten grass. If your dog appears to be healthy, a single vomiting incidence should not send you rushing to the vet. It may be nothing more than a simple upset stomach. Keep him away from any food for a few hours. You can allow him small amounts of water, but don't allow him to gulp water. Nothing makes a vomiting dog vomit more than a tummy full of water or food. If the problem persists, especially with puppies or old dogs, or if your dog has other symptoms, such as diarrhea, stomach bloating, listlessness, labored breathing, pain, or you see blood in the vomit or abnormal material, contact your veterinarian right away. And don't forget to take a sample of the vomit with you.

THE SENIOR BORDER COLLIE

Border Collies are considered "seniors" anywhere from age eight and older. You are the best judge of when to make this call for your dog. You will notice when he begins to slow down, is not interested in long walks around the neighborhood, sleeps more, seems to be getting gray around the muzzle, etc. Your veterinarian may also notice signs that indicate it is time to consider these your dog's golden years.

Many owners say that this time of their dog's life is the most enjoyable because their dogs have a routine, they know the family, and they know what to expect. Older dogs tend to be less active, which means you do not need to keep them as active, and they are more interested than ever in curling up in your lap!

Old age has its requirements, though, just as puppyhood did. You will need to assess your dog's overall health and determine what you will need to do to maintain it at its peak. This may mean changing his diet to one specially formulated for seniors. It may mean supplementing his food with certain vitamins, minerals, or herbs for improved skin condition or healthier joints. It may mean your dog needs to wear a sweater in cool weather and a coat when it's cold.

Mind how you interact with your senior citizen. His eyesight or hearing may be failing before it is readily apparent; be sure he hears and sees you when asking him to do things so you don't get upset with him. His bladder control may weaken, leading to accidents in the house. These are probably as upsetting to him as to you; have patience—remember, your friend won't live forever. Treasure him while you can!

Toxic Substances

Most homes are toxic hotspots filled with items that can inadvertently and accidentally harm your dog. Here is a sampling of a few of the most common toxic threats:

- Antifreeze (ethylene-glycol—a sweet-tasting liquid that is particularly attractive to dogs).
- Alcoholic drinks / liquor
- Batteries (i.e., for remote controls, cameras, toys—contain harsh chemicals that can cause severe damage to his mouth, stomach, and other internal organs)
- Chocolate (contains two deadly toxins: theobromine and caffeine)
- Fertilizers
- Garbage (rotting garbage is a concentrated source of bacteria, some of which produce dangerous toxins)
- Herbicides (weed killers, etc)
- Ice-melting or de-icing salts.
- Insecticides (snail and rat baits, etc)
- Lead (surfaces painted with lead-based paint—chairs, tables, walls, plumbing materials, fishing weights / lures)
- Medications (human meds—anti-inflammatories, acetaminophen, cold and flu medications, vitamin supplements, anti-depressants, etc.)
- Mothballs
- Plants—both indoor and outdoor

AKC BORDER COLLIE BREED STANDARD

Preamble: The Border Collie originated in the border country between Scotland and England where the shepherds' breeding selection was based on biddable stock sense and the ability to work long days on rugged terrain. As a result of this selective breeding, the Border Collie developed the unique working style of gathering and fetching the stock with wide sweeping outruns. The stock is then controlled with an intense gaze known as "eye", coupled with a stalking style of movement. This selective breeding over hundreds of years developed the Border Collie's intensity, energy and trainability which are features so important that they are equal to physical size and appearance. The Border Collie has extraordinary instinct and an uncanny ability to reason. One of its greatest assets is the ability to work out of sight of its master without commands. Breeding based on this working ability has made this breed the world's premier sheep herding dog, a job the Border Collie is still used for worldwide.

General Appearance: The Border Collie is a well balanced, medium-sized dog of athletic appearance, displaying style and agility in equal measure with soundness and strength. Its hard, muscular body conveys the impression of effortless movement and endless endurance. The Border Collie is extremely intelligent, with its keen, alert expression being a very important characteristic of the breed. Any aspect of structure or temperament that would impede the dog's ability to function as a herding dog should be severely faulted. The Border Collie is, and should remain, a natural and unspoiled true working sheep dog whose conformation is described herein. Honorable scars and broken teeth incurred in the line of duty are acceptable.

Size, Proportion, Substance: The height at the withers varies from 19" to 22" for males, 18" to 21" for females. The body, from prosternum to point of buttocks, is slightly longer than the height at the withers with the length to height ratio being approximately 10:9. Bone must be strong, medium being correct but lighter bone is preferred over heavy. Overall balance between height, length, weight and bone is crucial and is more important than any absolute measurement. Dogs must be presented in hard working condition. Excess body weight is not to be mistaken for muscle or substance. Any single feature of size appearing out of proportion should be considered a fault.

Head: Expression is intelligent, alert, eager, and full of interest. Eyes are set well apart, of moderate size, oval in shape. The color encompasses the full range of brown eyes, dogs having body colors other than black may have noticeably lighter eye color. Blue eyes (with one, both or part of one or both eyes being blue) in dogs other than merle, are acceptable but not preferred. Eye rims should be fully pigmented, lack thereof considered a fault according to degree. Ears are of medium size, set well apart, one or both carried erect and/or semi-erect (varying from 1/4 to 3/4 of the ear erect). When semi-erect, the tips may fall forward or outward to the side. Ears are sensitive and mobile. Skull is relatively flat and moderate in width. The skull and muzzle are approximately equal in length. In profile the top of the skull is parallel with the top of the muzzle. Stop moderate, but distinct. The muzzle is strong, tapering slightly to the nose. The underjaw is strong and well developed. A domed, blocky or very narrow skull is faulty according to degree, as is cheekiness and a snipey muzzle. Nose color matches the primary body color. Nostrils are well developed. Lack of nose pigmentation is a fault according to degree. Bite: Teeth and jaws are strong, meeting in a scissors bite. Complete dentition is required. Missing molars or pre-molars are serious faults as is an undershot or overshot bite.

Neck, Topline, Body: Neck is of proportional length to the body, strong and muscular, slightly arched and blending smoothly into the shoulders. Topline: Back is level from behind the withers to the slightly arched, muscular loins, falling to a gently sloping croup. Body is athletic in appearance with a deep, moderately broad chest reaching no further than the point of the elbow. The rib cage is moderately long with well sprung ribs. Loins moderately deep and short, muscular, slightly arched and with a slight but distinct tuck up. The tail is set on low and is moderately long with the bone reaching at least to the hock. The ideal tail carriage is low when the dog is concentrating on a given task and may have a slight upward swirl at the end like a shepherd's crook. In excitement, it may be raised proudly and waved like a banner, showing a confident personality. A tail curled over the back is a fault.

Forequarters: Forelegs should be parallel when viewed from front, pasterns slightly sloping when viewed from side. Because sufficient length of leg is crucial for the type of work the breed is required to do, the distance from the wither to the elbow is slightly less than from the elbow to the ground and legs that are too short in proportion to the rest of the body are a serious fault. The shoulder blades are long, well laid back and well-angulated to the upper arm. Shoulder blades and upper arms are equal in length. There is sufficient width between the tops of the shoulder blades to allow for the characteristic crouch when approaching and moving stock. The elbows are neither in nor out. Feet are compact, oval in shape; pads deep and strong, toes moderately arched and close together with strong nails of moderate length. Dewclaws may be removed.

Hindquarters: Broad and muscular, in profile sloping gracefully to the low set tail. The thighs are long, broad, deep and muscular. Stifles are well turned with strong hocks that may be either parallel or very slightly turned in. Dewclaws should be removed. Feet, although slightly smaller, are the same as front.

Coat: Two varieties are permissible, both having close-fitting, dense, weather resistant double coats with the top coat either straight or wavy and coarser in texture than the undercoat which is soft, short and dense. The rough variety is medium in length without being excessive. Forelegs, haunches, chest and underside are feathered and the coat on face, ears, feet, fronts of legs is short and smooth. The smooth variety is short over entire body, is usually coarser in texture than the rough variety and may have slight feathering on forelegs, haunches, chest and ruff. Neither coat type is preferred over the other. Seasonal shedding is normal and should not be penalized. The Border Collie's purpose as an actively working herding dog shall be clearly evident in its presentation. Excess hair on the feet, hock and pastern areas may be neatened for the show ring. Whiskers are untrimmed. Dogs that are overly groomed (trimmed and/or sculpted) should be penalized according to the extent.

Color: The Border Collie appears in all colors or combination of colors and/or markings. Solid color, bi-color, tri-color, merle and sable dogs are to be judged equally with no one color or pattern preferred over another. White markings may be clear white or ticked to any degree. Random white patches on the body and head are permissible but should not predominate. Color and markings are always secondary to physical evaluation and gait.

Gait: The Border Collie is an agile dog, able to suddenly change speed and direction while maintaining balance and grace. Endurance is its trademark. The Border Collie's most used working gaits are the gallop and a moving crouch (stealth) which convert to a balanced and free trot, with minimum lift of the feet. The head is carried level with or slightly below the withers. When shown, Border Collies should move on a loose lead and at moderate speed, never raced around the ring with the head held high. When viewed from the side the trot is not long striding, yet covers the ground with minimum effort, exhibiting facility of movement rather than a hard driving action. Exaggerated reach and drive at the trot are not useful to the Border Collie. The topline is firm. Viewed from the front, action is forward and true without wasted motion. Viewed from the rear, hindquarters drive with thrust and flexibility with hocks turning neither in nor out, moving close together but never touching. The legs, both front and rear, tend to converge toward the center line as speed increases. Any deficiency that detracts from efficient movement is a fault.

Temperament: The Border Collie is energetic, intelligent, keen, alert, and responsive. An intense worker of great tractability, it is affectionate towards friends but may be sensibly reserved towards strangers. When approached, the Border Collie should stand its ground. It should be alert and interested, never showing fear, dullness or resentment. Any tendencies toward viciousness, nervousness or shyness are very serious faults.

Faults: Any deviation from the foregoing should be considered a fault, the seriousness of the fault depending upon the extent of the deviation.

Approved: January 13, 2004
Effective: March 2, 2004

KENNEL CLUB BREED STANDARD

General Appearance: Well proportioned, smooth outline showing quality, gracefulness and perfect balance, combined with sufficient substance to give impression of endurance. Any tendency to coarseness or weediness undesirable.

Characteristics: Tenacious, hard-working sheep dog, of great tractability.

Temperament: Keen, alert, responsive and intelligent. Neither nervous nor aggressive.

Head and Skull: Skull fairly broad, occiput not pronounced. Cheeks not full or rounded. Muzzle, tapering to nose, moderately short and strong. Skull and foreface approximately equal in length. Stop very distinct. Nose black, except in brown or chocolate colour when it may be brown. In blues nose should be slate colour. Nostrils well developed.

Eyes: Set wide apart, oval-shaped, of moderate size, brown in colour except in merles where one or both or part of one or both may be blue. Expression mild, keen, alert and intelligent.

Ears: Medium size and texture, set well apart. Carried erect or semi-erect and sensitive in use.

Mouth: Teeth and jaws strong with a perfect, regular and complete scissor bite, i.e. upper teeth closely overlapping lower teeth and set square to the jaws.

Neck: Of good length, strong and muscular, slightly arched and broadening to shoulders.

Forequarters: Front legs parallel when viewed from front, pasterns slightly sloping when viewed from side. Bone strong but not heavy. Shoulders well laid back, elbows close to body.

Body: Athletic in appearance, ribs well sprung, chest deep and rather broad, loins deep and muscular, but not tucked up. Body slightly longer than height at shoulder.

Hindquarters: Broad, muscular, in profile sloping gracefully to set on of tail. Thighs long, deep and muscular with well turned stifles and strong well let down hocks. From hock to ground, hindlegs well boned and parallel when viewed from rear.

Feet: Oval, pads deep, strong and sound, toes arched and close together. Nails short and strong.

Tail: Moderately long, the bone reaching at least to hock, set on low, well furnished and with an upward swirl towards the end, completing graceful contour and balance of dog. Tail may be raised in excitement, never carried over back.

Gait/Movement: Free, smooth and tireless, with minimum lift of feet, conveying impression of ability to move with great stealth and speed.

Coat: Two varieties: 1) Moderately long; 2) Smooth. In both, topcoat dense and medium textured, undercoat soft and dense giving good weather resistance. In moderately long-coated variety, abundant coat forms mane, breeching and brush. On face, ears, forelegs (except for feather), hindlegs from hock to ground, hair should be short and smooth.

Colour: Variety of colours permissible. White should never predominate.

Size: Ideal height: dogs: 53 cms (21 ins); bitches slightly less.

Faults: Any departure from the foregoing points should be considered a fault and the seriousness with which the fault should be regarded should be in exact proportion to its degree and its effect upon the health and welfare of the dog.

Note: Male animals should have two apparently normal testicles fully descended into the scrotum.

March 1994

ASSOCIATIONS AND ORGANIZATIONS

Breed Clubs

American Border Collie Association
Patty Rogers, Secretary
82 Rogers Road
Perkinston, MS 39573-8843
Telephone: (601) 928-7551
Fax: (601) 928-5148
E-mail: ABCA@datasync.com
www.americanbordercollie.org

American Herding Breed Association
www.ahba-herding.org

American Kennel Club (AKC)
5580 Centerview Drive
Raleigh, NC 27606
Telephone: (919) 233-9767
Fax: (919) 233-3627
E-mail: info@akc.org
www.akc.org

Border Collie Society of America
Laura Wright, Corresponding Secretary
2005 Sussex Drive
Mt. Dora, FL 32757
www.bordercolliesociety.com

Canadian Border Collie Association
Werner Reitboeck, Secretary
Box 424
Winchester, Ontario, Canada
K0C 2K0,
Telephone: (613) 448-3817
Fax: (613) 448-3265
E-mail: registrar@
canadianbordercollies.org
www.canadianbordercollies.org

Canadian Kennel Club (CKC)
89 Skyway Avenue, Suite 100
Etobicoke, Ontario M9W 6R4
Telephone: (416) 675-5511
Fax: (416) 675-6506
E-mail: information@ckc.ca
www.ckc.ca

Federation Cynologique Internationale (FCI)
Secretariat General de la FCI
Place Albert 1er, 13
B – 6530 Thuin
Belqique
www.fci.be

International Sheep Dog Society (ISDS)
Clifton House
4a Goldington Road
Bedford
MK40 3NF
Telephone: 44 (0) 1234 352672
Fax: 44 (0) 1234 348214
E-mail: OFFICE@ISDS.ORG.
UK
www.isds.org.uk

The Kennel Club
1 Clarges Street
London
W1J 8AB
Telephone: 0870 606 6750
Fax: 0207 518 1058
www.the-kennel-club.org.uk

North American SheepDog Society (NASDS)
Robin Reasoner, Acting Secretary
E-mail: nasds@
midwestherding.com

United Kennel Club (UKC)
100 E. Kilgore Road
Kalamazoo, MI 49002-5584
Telephone: (269) 343-9020
Fax: (269) 343-7037
E-mail: pbickell@ukcdogs.com
www.ukcdogs.com

United States Border Collie Club (USBCC)
www.bordercollie.org/club

United States Border Collie Handler's Association
Francis Raley, Secretary
2915 Anderson Lane
Crawford, TX 76638
Telpehone: (254) 486-2500
Fax: (254) 486-2271
E-mail: f.raley@worldnet.att.net
www.usbcha.com

Pet Sitters

National Association of Professional Pet Sitters
15000 Commerce Parkway,
Suite C
Mt. Laurel, New Jersey 08054
Telephone: (856) 439-0324
Fax: (856) 439-0525
E-mail: napps@ahint.com
www.petsitters.org

Pet Sitters International
201 East King Street
King, NC 27021-9161
Telephone: (336) 983-9222
Fax: (336) 983-5266
E-mail: info@petsit.com
www.petsit.com

Rescue Organizations and Animal Welfare Groups

American Humane Association (AHA)
63 Inverness Drive East
Englewood, CO 80112
Telephone: (303) 792-9900
Fax: 792-5333
www.americanhumane.org

American Society for the Prevention of Cruelty to Animals (ASPCA)
424 E. 92nd Street
New York, NY 10128-6804
Telephone: (212) 876-7700
www.aspca.org

**Royal Society for the
Prevention of Cruelty to
Animals (RSPCA)**
Telephone: 0870 3335 999
Fax: 0870 7530 284
www.rspca.org.uk

**The Humane Society of the
United States (HSUS)**
2100 L Street, NW
Washington DC 20037
Telephone: (202) 452-1100
www.hsus.org

Sports

**Canine Freestyle Federation,
Inc.**
Secretary: Brandy Clymire
E-Mail: secretary@canine-
freestyle.org
www.canine-freestyle.org

**International Agility Link
(IAL)**
Global Administrator: Steve
Drinkwater
E-mail: yunde@powerup.au
www.agilityclick.com/~ial

**North American Dog
Agility Council**
11522 South Hwy 3
Cataldo, ID 83810
www.nadac.com

**North American Flyball
Association**
www.flyball.org
1400 West Devon Avenue
#512
Chicago, IL 6066
800-318-6312

**United States Dog Agility
Association**
P.O. Box 850955
Richardson, TX 75085-0955
Telephone: (972) 487-2200
www.usdaa.com

**World Canine Freestyle
Organization**
P.O. Box 350122
Brooklyn, NY 11235-2525
Telephone: (718) 332-8336
www.worldcaninefreestyle.org

Therapy

Delta Society
875 124th Ave NE, Suite 101
Bellevue, WA 98005
Telephone: (425) 226-7357
Fax: (425) 235-1076
E-mail: info@deltasociety.org
www.deltasociety.org

Therapy Dogs Incorporated
PO Box 5868
Cheyenne, WY 82003
Telephone: (877) 843-7364
E-mail: therdog@sisna.com
www.therapydogs.com

**Therapy Dogs International
(TDI)**
88 Bartley Road
Flanders, NJ 07836
Telephone: (973) 252-9800
Fax: (973) 252-7171
E-mail: tdi@gti.net
www.tdi-dog.org

Training

**Association of Pet Dog
Trainers (APDT)**
150 Executive Center Drive
Box 35
Greenville, SC 29615
Telephone: (800) PET-DOGS
Fax: (864) 331-0767
E-mail: information@apdt.com
www.apdt.com

**National Association of Dog
Obedience Instructors**
PMB 369
729 Grapevine Hwy.
Hurst, TX 76054-2085
www.nadoi.org

Veterinary and
Health Resources

**Academy of Veterinary
Homeopathy (AVH)**
P.O. Box 9280
Wilmington, DE 19809
Telephone: (866) 652-1590
Fax: (866) 652-1590
E-mail: office@TheAVH.org
www.theavh.org

**American Academy of
Veterinary Acupuncture
(AAVA)**
100 Roscommon Drive, Suite
320
Middletown, CT 06457
Telephone: (860) 635-6300
Fax: (860) 635-6400
E-mail: office@aava.org
www.aava.org

**American Animal Hospital
Association (AAHA)**
P.O. Box 150899
Denver, CO 80215-0899
Telephone: (303) 986-2800
Fax: (303) 986-1700
E-mail: info@aahanet.org
www.aahanet.org/index.cfm

**American College of
Veterinary Internal Medicine
(ACVIM)**
1997 Wadsworth Blvd.,
Suite A
Lakewood, CO 80214-5293
Telephone: (800) 245-9081
Fax: (303) 231-0880
E-mail: ACVIM@ACVIM.org
www.acvim.org

**American College
of Veterinary
Ophthalmologists (ACVO)**
P.O. Box 1311
Meridian, Idaho 83860
Telephone: (208) 466-7624
Fax: (208) 466-7693
E-mail: office@acvo.com
www.acvo.com

American Holistic Veterinary Medical Association (AHVMA)
2218 Old Emmorton Road
Bel Air, MD 21015
Telephone: (410) 569-0795
Fax: (410) 569-2346
E-mail: office@ahvma.org
www.ahvma.org

American Veterinary Medical Association (AVMA)
1931 North Meacham Road
– Suite 100
Schaumburg, IL 60173
Telephone: (847) 925-8070
Fax: (847) 925-1329
E-mail: avmainfo@avma.org
www.avma.org

ASPCA Animal Poison Control Center
1717 South Philo Road, Suite 36
Urbana, IL 61802
Telephone: (888) 426-4435
www.aspca.org

British Veterinary Association (BVA)
7 Mansfield Street
London
W1G 9NQ
Telephone: 020 7636 6541
Fax: 020 7436 2970
E-mail: bvahq@bva.co.uk
www.bva.co.uk

Canine Eye Registration Foundation (CERF)
VMDB/CERF
1248 Lynn Hall
625 Harrison St.
Purdue University
West Lafayette, IN 47907-2026
Telephone: (765) 494-8179
E-mail: CERF@vmbd.org
www.vmdb.org

Orthopedic Foundation for Animals (OFA)
2300 NE Nifong Blvd
Columbus, Missouri 65201-3856
Telephone: (573) 442-0418
Fax: (573) 875-5073
Email: ofa@offa.org
www.offa.org

PUBLICATIONS

AKC *Family Dog*
American Kennel Club
260 Madison Avenue
New York, NY 10016
Telephone: (800) 490-5675
E-mail: familydog@akc.org
www.akc.org/pubs/familydog

AKC *Gazette*
American Kennel Club
260 Madison Avenue
New York, NY 10016
Telephone: (800) 533-7323
E-mail: gazette@akc.org
www.akc.org/pubs/gazette

Dog & Kennel
Pet Publishing, Inc.
7-L Dundas Circle
Greensboro, NC 27407
Telephone: (336) 292-4272
Fax: (336) 292-4272
E-mail: info@petpublishing.com
www.dogandkennel.com

Dog Fancy
Subscription Department
P.O. Box 53264
Boulder, CO 80322-3264
Telephone: (800) 365-4421
E-mail: barkback@dogfancy.com
www.dogfancy.com

Dogs Monthly
Ascot House
High Street, Ascot,
Berkshire SL5 7JG
United Kingdom
Telephone: 0870 730 8433
Fax: 0870 730 8431
E-mail: admin@rtc-associates.freeserve.co.uk
www.corsini.co.uk/dogsmonthly

ACKNOWLEDGEMENTS

A special thanks to my husband, Paul, whose love and encouragement have been the constant in my life, enabling me to the opportunity to write and train dogs every day. Special thanks to Patrick Shannahan, Denise Wall, and Dr. LeRoy Boyd for their time and expertise; Linda Rorem for her historical research and for unselfishly sharing her knowledge; Louis Irigaray, and the relatives of Andrew Little and Dominque Laxalt for sharing their time, dog stories, and family heritage; Victoria Schneider for her grooming expertise; Colin Sealy at the Kennel Club (UK) and the people at the International Sheep Dog Society for their research; and all of the interesting and remarkable Border Collie owners I have had the good fortune to speak with along the way. There have been so many that to mention them all would fill an entire book. To Bobbie Anderson and Sylvia Bishop for their training, insight and words of wisdom through the years, and to Heather Russell-Revesz at TFH Publications, Inc., for her guidance.

ABOUT THE AUTHOR

Tracy Libby is an award-winning freelance writer and author of *Building Blocks for Performance* (Alpine 2002). Her articles have appeared in numerous publications, including the *AKC Gazette, Puppies USA, You and Your Dog, and Dog Fancy's Popular Dogs series.* She is a member of the Dog Writers Association of America and a recipient of the Ellsworth S. Howell award for distinguished dog writing. She lives in Oregon, and has been involved in the sport of dogs for 21 years, exhibiting in conformation and obedience.

PHOTO CREDITS